I KNOW YOU'RE

OUT THERE

I KNOW YOU'RE

OUT THERE

Private Longings, Public Humiliations,

and Other Tales from the Personals

MICHAEL BEAUMIER

THREE RIVERS PRESS
NEW YORK

Library of Congress Cataloging-in-Publication Data
Beaumier, Michael.
I know you're out there: private longings, public humiliations,
and other tales from the personals / Michael Beaumier.— 1st ed.
1. Dating (Social customs) 2. Interpersonal relations. I. Title.
HQ801.B353 2006
306.7302'07—dc22
2006009266

ISBN-13: 978-0-307-33809-9
ISBN-10: 0-307-33809-6

Printed in the United States of America

Design by *Maria Elias*

10 9 8 7 6 5 4 3 2 1

First Edition

For
Anaheed and Ira
and for
Jerry Klein

The Awful Truth

The stories contained herein are true. *True.* Real, genuine, actual, valid, authentic, bona fide, sincere—not fake. None of this has been made up. You deserve the truth, and you're going to get it.

However.

There are times when the truth is just too horrible to stomach. Believe me, I know. The truth is an awful thing: messy, cumbersome— and often embarrassing. And it is for this reason that the characters, correspondences, and conversations presented in this slim volume, insofar as they relate to the personals, have been altered.

This is not lying; it is simply my nature to protect the innocent— and also the guilty. I try not to play favorites. Personals advertisers, as they are presented here, are composites of real people, with healthy doses of whimsy and nihilism thrown in, and no particular person's identity or circumstances is intended nor should be inferred. This book is not about you.

Contents

I KNOW YOU'RE

OUT THERE

[1] *Meant for Each Other*

*SWF LOOKING FOR you, a slim, attractive, kind, honest
and generous man who understands the value of hard work,
loves his family and hopes to meet a special lady. I bring
sweetness and a true heart to the table. Mid-40s or older. Let
me hear from you.*

People like to say it's the little things that'll end a relationship, but those
people are amateurs. Being sentenced to prison, excusing oneself to go
get cigarettes and never returning, the ill-timed discovery that one's
beloved is attracted to another gender or species—*those* are little things.
They are nothing compared to having every single moment of your
daily existence—every detail, every gesture, everything you say or do or
think—be a point of contention. Let me explain. I am apparently hard
to live with. I have been told this, repeatedly. I smoke, I swear, I dress
badly, I snore and steal blankets, I make too much noise in the bathroom
and forget to flush, I wash whites with darks, and I chew loudly. I
inspire neither tender words nor sweet nothings, only criticisms and

complaints. *Don't leave hair in the sink. Be nice to my mother. For the last time, put the seat down.* Sheesh. You'd think the person who's supposed to know me better than anybody wouldn't have so many questions. Why do I always buy yellow mustard when I've been told a million times to get honey dijon? Why do I constantly turn the thermostat down when it's cold outside, and up when it's warm? Why am I so cheap? Why am I so quiet? And why do I look so mad all the time?

This is what love can turn into. Pettiness, cruelty, unhappiness, taking little digs at each other, playing cruel mind games and having spats, trotting out every instance of betrayal and hurt in order to score points in a game neither one of us understands or could possibly win. This is what happens after the bliss gets threadbare, as bliss inevitably must. Every word comes out sounding hostile and sarcastic; we can't even clear our throats without one of us demanding to know just what the hell the other one means by *that* crack.

Things are tough at home. We're in our ninth consecutive year of breaking up in the most bitter and unpleasant manner imaginable, a new personal best for me, though I don't feel particularly proud. People can find love and be happy-ever-after, I know this, I've seen it on television and in the movies; I've even had it in my own life. We were happy, at first—playing house, making dinner together, holding hands and talking for hours and hours, blissfully unaware of the time and the disaster that awaited us. But, sadly, the word *honeymoon* is nearly inevitably, practically always, followed by the word *over*. Now our mutual unhappiness and inability to actually end this agony are the only aspects of life in which we've proven to be compatible. We're both equally miserable, and we both desperately want to play the victim, we have that in common, but lately it has occurred to me that these are, perhaps, not enough reasons upon which to base a long-term relationship. We know we can't go on like this forever. Fighting has become exhausting and only occasionally exhilarating, and lately the old thrill of raising voices over the gas bill or nearly coming to blows over taking out the garbage is gone. We're in one of those phases where I sleep on the couch—it's been every night for the past two years, by mutual agreement; we may go to bed angry, but at least we get some sleep. In our waking hours, we go on and on, sniping and fighting, every morning and every night. In between, I go to work.

At work, all the bad stuff fades away, all the bitterness and hostility and unhappiness. At work, there is love. *Love.* From nine to five, it's unavoidable. There is love, and romance and passion and hope, and chemistry and rapport and delight, and hot mind-numbing sex so incredible that your bones vibrate afterward, and no one criticizing anyone's cooking skills or mismatched socks or the way one hangs the toilet paper. Ah, work. It's pure bliss, I tell you.

I love my job. I love the subway ride every morning through the bowels of Chicago, I love opening the door of the building I work in, I love climbing the steps to my office and finding the stack of personal ads waiting for me on my desk, each a tale of joy and woe, and I love that my phone is ringing before I even sit down, before I can get that first cup of coffee.

"But I don't know what to say," the woman on the other end of the phone tells me. I hear this several times every day. "I just don't want to sound like a pathetic loser, you know?"

"Lady," I tell her, "me neither."

Admission: I work in the personals. If you're confused, I understand. Back in the old days, before computers and cell phones and speed dating and singles clubs, the personals were the most efficient and safe way to meet people. Need a date? Write a personal. Looking for a husband or a wife? Place an ad. I can help you find a bridge partner, a mistress, someone with whom to both carpool and indulge in your strange balloon fetish, just tell me what you want. You still see personals these days, strange little ads filled with strange little abbreviations usually found in the back pages of newspapers, where they do no harm and attract little attention; you'd miss them unless you were really looking. Personals are noteworthy mostly for the strange code they're written in, a cacophony of capital letters and staccato, rat-tat-tat descriptions that somehow or other translate into someone's deepest longings or darkest desires—like this:

SWF 38 sks SM35–50 for LTR. Be nsmk, fit, D/D-free, urb.
dwell, no chld.

In English, this translates as "Single white female, age thirty-eight, seeks single male, thirty-five to fifty years old, for long-term relationship. You must be a nonsmoker, fit, drug- and disease-free, urban dweller, and have no children." See? It's easy. Once you've picked up the basics, it's really very simple. Of course, this is only a start; it's one thing to say what you want, but it's quite another to *get* what you want. And that's where I come in.

Working in the personals isn't all glamorous fun—it isn't a cushy job, like writing obituaries. An obituary, like a personal ad, is something that happens when everything else fails and you have nothing left to lose, but the resemblance ends there. Those obituary guys have it made, because their people aren't nearly as needy as mine. Nobody calls them to complain that their obituary makes them sound too desperate. Obituaries have all the legitimacy and gravitas that the personals lack: being dead is awful, but it's better than the shame of being lonely.

People have a hard time believing that there's a person who actually works in the personals; what's more, once they get to know me, they have a hard time believing that person would be *me*. I understand. The irony of a guy in my particular romantic circumstances being the go-to man for fulfilling the heart's desire of an entire city is apparent on the face of it. The expectation is that I would be a hard, bitter, jaded cynic who has long since taken to drinking heavily. But, strangely, I'm not and I haven't. I believe in love. Not having love just makes my need to believe in it that much stronger.

"I'm not unattractive," she tells me. "Though, sure, I know I could stand to lose a few pounds. I have a job, and friends, and a life—but I don't want to oversell myself, either." I'm helping her sum up her personality in fifty to a hundred words, to appear in the back of a newspaper. If you've never tried it, it's actually a tricky kind of writing to do. Listing what's good about you can be incredibly dull, and can also accidentally make you seem slightly insane or at least very egotistical. The hesitant woman on the phone could be a morbidly obese shut-in living with the corpse of her insane mother, or possibly a kittenish bikini model-slash-Ph.D. student in biomechanical engineering; it's hard to tell. She wants to quote sonnets and drop cute lines from popular love songs, because that's what she thinks love is. She doesn't want to talk about *herself*. Most people are like this. She's blowing a golden opportunity, but it's really hard to explain that to her.

While I coax her to list all her attributes—her lustrous hair, her winning smile, her love of jazz and dark chocolate—I look over a fresh stack of ads. Two suburban divorcees with kids. A guy looking to get spanked. Some woman placing an ad for "a friend." An older man, he says mid-fifties, claims to look mid-forties, but I'm guessing probably mid-sixties, seeking a good time and making a veiled offer of compensation to any "comely, vivacious younger gals who might be reading this." Some people are vague, intentionally so, writing ads filled with clichés and platitudes that could apply to practically anyone, but some are so specific that I haven't the slightest idea what they're talking about. None of them knows what will work, but they are all trying.

"There are two things you need to do," I tell the mystery woman on the phone. "You've told me what you want and that's good, but you also need to tell me who you *are*. I know, it's not as easy as it sounds, but basically that's all there is to it."

Of course it's trite to say this—but so what? I'm actually interested in who she might be, and not just because I'm paid to ask. After all, I'm not paid very much, but besides that, I know what it's like to be overlooked and ignored. I know how hard it is to get someone, anyone, to stop and take notice, to pay attention, to actually see who you really are. Even the most docile and unassuming among us has a good story they're just dying to tell, an opinion to express, a point of view, but it's hard to find an audience when everyone's so into themselves—their own problems, their own lives. Every week there are three or four hundred new advertisers, and while most of them will never realize I'm here, or contemplate what I must think, those who do demand my complete attention. And I oblige.

This is, perhaps, the reason I'm good at this job: I know how to shut up and listen. I'm sure I don't have any other qualifications to speak of—no Ph.D. in clinical psychology, no degree in social work or behavioral sciences, no prescription pad, nothing that you'd assume would come in handy. There's no certification in matchmaking, nor professional associations, not even a support group. Journalism schools don't bother with the personals, and neither graduating from college nor flunking out of graduate school prepared me in any way for this career. It wasn't my lifelong aspiration to do this; I didn't spend my formative childhood years dreaming up clever ways to abbreviate. I just needed a job, and this was a job that nobody wanted. It's as if we were meant for each other.

I got the job, I assume, because I was the least crazy of everybody else they interviewed, but no one seems to remember exactly. I've been doing this for a long, long time—so long that people don't seem to recall that there was a time when I wasn't here. But everyone agrees now that I'm the right guy for the job, although there's little consensus as to why that is.

Is it stamina? I've certainly developed a strong stomach for all the stupid romantic clichés, and I've made my peace with them—though I'd like, for once, someone who says they're looking for a "partner in crime" to *really* be looking for a partner in crime—someone with a taste for film noir who can drive a getaway car or provide cover fire. Or am I just naturally sympathetic? It took a while to learn how to cope with people who are very bitter, or desperate, or both; the trick is to have enough tact to not point such things out to these folks. Maybe it's that I have a somewhat more open-minded view of human relations than most people. I don't discriminate based on age, gender, race, class, religion, nationality, education, and, I'm sure, a few thousand other things I can't think of off the top of my head—how could *I* possibly stand in judgment? The woman babbling on the phone, the people whose ads sit before me in a neat little pile—they all think doing this means that they've reached the bottom of the barrel, the end of the rope, and that they've gone as low as they can go. But you can't be generous out of pity. I honestly envy them a little, and admire them a lot. They're still fighting and hoping, while I'm pushing the disappointment and disillusionment of my own love life to the back of my mind, grateful for the chance to come to work, get outside myself, and listen to someone else.

Besides, I can't act high and mighty. It's bad for business. And I don't want to lose my job—it's the only thing I'm good at. I once wrote a personal ad for a Russian émigré lesbian Orthodox Jew with only the barest English skills and corrected the atrocious spelling of a pair of identical-twin swingers from the south side of town on the same day, before lunch. It's fun like that, all the time, every day.

The poor, shy woman on the phone, the one who didn't know what to say, has been talking nonstop for more than ten minutes, and in that time I've heard all about her bike ride last summer through the south of France, how she cried when her pet ferret died, and that she's allergic to peanuts but still loves peanut butter. Being a gentleman, I've said very little. Most of the time I'm so quiet, people don't even realize that I'm there, which is how I prefer it. After all, this isn't about *me*.

That's another reason why I love this job. It reminds me that love means knowing it's never, ever, *ever* about you. If her personal ad works—and I give no guarantees—this woman will learn, like all the others, that love isn't at all the thing they say it is in poetry or romance novels or movies. The thing about being in love, I think, is that while it's about two people, it's never just about you. It's listening more than talking, or at least it's supposed to be. If she's lucky, this will be the last time she ever gets to get a word in edgewise. She and her beloved, wherever and whoever he may be, will compete for attention from each other day and night, fighting for the pleasures of hearing and being heard.

Ferrets. France. Peanut butter. This is what she has to offer. It's a good start, and we write up an advertisement and hope for the best. She still wants to talk of love, of stars and birds and flighty, gooey things, but I need my coffee. I always try to be diplomatic, but it's very hard to keep your patience when complete strangers continually try to shove greeting-card sentimentalities down your throat. Every day it's nothing but *love* this and *love* that, with an occasional appearance of *lust* to break the monotony, and a half hour for lunch. You'd think the subject of love had been exhausted by now. You'd think people would know better than to try stating the case anew, but you would be wrong.

*   *   *

If I were the one writing a personal ad—an ad for myself—what would I say? I get asked this a lot. Most of the time I beg off, or change the subject, or laugh derisively and declare that personal ads are strictly for losers. But in truth, I just don't know what *I* would say. I'm not sure there's anything *to* say. Love is the thing that everybody's looking for, even when we know it's hard to find, and I know that finding it is a cakewalk compared to living with it, and the only thing worse than living with it is losing it. Love is this big thing that makes us look so small when we crawl up next to it, it leaves us wide-eyed and speechless. But I have absolutely nothing of use to say when it comes to the subject of love. People shouldn't ask me. I have a terrible track record, and mostly I prefer to just listen to others talk about it.

"I know you're out there!" she exclaims, and she's thrilled with her choice, no doubt thinking she's the first person ever to combine those words in such a perfect fashion. "And be sure to include the exclamation point," she tells me, and I dutifully comply. For me, these words come across as a little ominous, even when decorated with an exclamation point, but I keep the thought to myself.

She thanks me, profusely and honestly, for my help. I do not warn her of what she might be in for, the things that will happen as she looks for love and everything that follows when she finds it. She thinks I'm wonderful and kind, and I don't argue. But she doesn't know what I'm getting from this. When I'm at work, I get to think about love. I get to believe in love. And when I get home I'll inevitably be asked, out of courtesy more than real interest, "What happened at work today?" And I'll answer, as I always do, "Oh, nothing." Anything else wouldn't make sense, and none of it would be understood anyhow.

[2] *Losers*

WE'RE A BUNCH of high-powered mid-career derivative finance people forming an exciting social group to study the applications of neural network methodologies to probability theory, statistics and financial modeling. Sounds like fun? Join us for friendship, camaraderie, good time and plenty of math.

Every week I do business with three or four hundred brand-new people, and no matter who they are—rich or poor, young or old, black or white, male or female—they are all mortified at having to write a personal ad to find a date. There is no greater shame, apparently, than to advertise the longings of your heart as if you were throwing a garage sale, putting your hopes and dreams out for strangers to pick apart and haggle over. The personals feel dirty, unseemly, pathetic—and for the inexperienced and uninitiated, writing that first ad seems like a humiliating admission of total failure.

Luckily, there's me—I'm here to help, with a kindly word and an open heart, providing tender encouragement to the nervous newbie. Buck up, lonely hearts! All you need is a big-hearted someone to gently ease you into the fun and exciting world of personal ads—someone to guide and support you, someone who *cares*. And I, by default and by virtue of paycheck, am that someone. So here's a primer of sorts, a brief introduction to everything you need to know about placing your very own personal ad:

Nobody Loves You

Admitting you have a problem is the first step to beating it, right? Okay, maybe I'm thinking of heroin, but regardless—nobody loves you. I'm sorry, but it's true. Why else would you be here? Of course, just because nobody loves you doesn't mean you shouldn't be loved— far from it! You've taken an important first step by considering a personal advertisement, and if it's any consolation, you aren't alone. Look at all the people who place personals—there are pages and pages of them each and every week. Nobody loves them, either. You aren't so special after all, are you? And you're not nearly as unlovable as some of these people, believe me. Take this fine lady, for example:

> *HYPNOTIZED GUYS TURN me on. Let me put you in a trance. SWF amateur hypnotist looking for guys to put under. Can be sexual or not. ISO guys with open minds, height/ weight proportional, picture required.*

Isn't that sad? Hypnotism, magic spells, kidnapping, free dinners— people will do the most awful, desperate things to get someone to love them. All you're doing is asking. There. Don't you feel better now?

Everybody Hates You

It's not enough that nobody loves you. That's only a start. If you really want this personal-ad thing to work, you have to be willing to let people *hate* you. The biggest mistake people make is to avoid letting anyone hate them—they think, "Jeepers, I don't want to miss out on finding the man/woman/other of my dreams, so I'd better be on my best behavior and avoid saying anything that will tick off someone who might be perfectly perfect for me." People shy away from the controversial, the incendiary, all the hot-button topics that make them unique but possibly unpopular. First-timers have a tendency to avoid admitting their religious beliefs or disbeliefs, keep quiet about their political leanings and prejudices, and behave themselves to the point where they're nothing but piles of decorum, sweetness, and mush. Sometimes they even go so far as to offer up versions of themselves that couldn't possibly be true:

> *CHAUVINIST SEEKS AMENDS. Lonely SWM 28 hopes to learn to treat women better from young professional ladies. I am honest and loyal, just misguided. I will cook and clean, I will obey. Let me repay you for my wrongs to others, and learn for the future. Meet me for lunch.*

I don't buy it, and you shouldn't either. Twenty-eight is a little old to suddenly have such a dramatic change of heart, don't you think? You know if you go out with this guy, you'll be scrubbing his toilet and fetching his slippers within a matter of weeks.

Just go ahead and put it out there—if you believe, deep in your heart, that a woman's place is in the home, barefoot and pregnant and kept away from the voting booth, go ahead and say so. If you think voting Republican is a crime that merits bringing back the hallowed tradition of public flogging, don't keep mum. All the awful things you'd prefer to hide about yourself—your kleptomania, your commitment to Satanism, your three adorable cats—are parts of *who you actually are.* The whole personal-ad setup is more or less anonymous, so what's stopping you? This guy surely wasn't afraid of how he might come across:

> *BY THE YEAR 2020 I will have slept with over six thousand women. Currently I'm on number eight. Stunning male with great potential for evening activities seeking several thousand someones who want to go out once and enjoy a casual screw.*

Sure, this fellow may not get many dates, but at least the ones he will get will know what he's all about. At the very least he's gotten your attention, even if you disagree with him—which is better than being ignored.

You're Not Fooling Anybody

You are so very clever, aren't you? You think you can fool people with your subtle choice of words, or your innocent omission of detail—but I have news for you, babycakes: it's been done before, it's been done better, and it's been done to death. Everyone knows that when you say *college-educated* you don't necessarily mean *college-graduated,* and claiming your weight is proportionate to your height is utterly meaningless, when you think about it.

People aren't as dumb as you think they are. People aren't even as dumb as *I* think they are. Women say things that they think will fool men, and men say things that they think will fool women—but the fact is, men and women have this terrible habit of fooling only themselves.

WHAT WOMEN SAY	*WHAT MEN HEAR*
Adventurous	Slutty
Athletic	Flat-chested
Average-looking	Ugly
Beautiful	Delusional
Contagious smile	Drug addict
Emotionally secure	Heavily medicated
Fortyish	Forty-nine
Free spirit	Junkie
Fun	Annoying
Old-fashioned	Closed-minded
Open-minded	Desperate
Outgoing	Loud and obnoxious
Rubenesque	Grossly fat
Voluptuous	Hugely fat
Young at heart	Old

WHAT MEN SAY	WHAT WOMEN HEAR
Athletic	Watches football on TV
Average-looking	Hair on ears, nose, back
Educated	Patronizing
Fortyish	Fifty-two
Friendship first	Sex required
Fun	Drunk
Good-looking	Dumb
Honest	Liar
Huggable	Fat
Likes to cuddle	Mama's boy
Mature	Old
Poet	Writes bathroom graffiti
Sensitive	Gay
Very sensitive	Very gay
Stable	Charged, but acquitted

Get Over Yourself

The personals aren't for spineless wimps. You want to whine and bitch about how sad this all is? Fine. But don't do it on my dime or time, buddy. If you think writing personal ads is a hard, bitter, terrible experience, just think about what it must be like for me to read them. A little sympathy would be nice. I might love this job, but you don't know that unless I tell you.

When you let go of all the nonsense, when you let loose and say who you are and what you want and how you want it, you'll not only find what you're looking for but you'll entertain *me* in the process—and that's saying something. The following are some of the more entertaining, if somewhat disturbing, ads I've come across:

CIVIL WAR RE-CREATIONIST ISO SWM 18–30 for illicit role-play. I am a Northern soldier, possibly with leg injury. You, a Rebel in every sense of the word. If you can capture me, you can have me. Accurate description, no fatties, costume helpful. No fatties! Call, and let's duel it out!

DESPERATELY SEEKING DINNER. Charming SAF ISO dining sugar daddy for upscale culinary experience. Must be willing to pay for my meal, and be handsome enough to keep my food down. You get the pleasure of my company and the chance to see my mouth with a fork in it. Bon appétit. For me.

BLACK MALE LOOKING for soft angora-wearing woman to have sexual fun. Must have soft, fuzzy hair. Only kinky women should respond. You must be very naughty, but love to wear angora sweaters, and your hair must be very, very soft.

I do want to add, however, that if you are one of these people who insists on wallowing in your weirdness—if you absolutely cannot help but wrap yourself up in humiliation and embarrassment and let your freak flag fly—all I can suggest is that you pick another venue. There's a place where you can go to be yourself that's far more anonymous than the personals, and it's called the Internet. Think about it—won't you? A guy can take only so many freaks in one day.

[3] *Means of Introduction*

READING AYN RAND on the subway, Monday evening. I sat beside you for a few stops to Diversey, where you got off. I was in shorts and flip-flops. You're that girl who goes to my gym, I think. I didn't say much, but the memory of your beautiful eyes makes me wish I had. Would just like to talk. Just talk. I'm sensitive and funny, and I absolutely believe there is someone somewhere waiting for me. Is it you?

Bill wanted to place a personal ad. He'd seen a woman, a beautiful woman he couldn't forget, at a bar called Gamekeepers the Saturday evening before. Gamekeepers is a semi-quasi-sportish kind of bar in a solidly gentrified part of Chicago, the kind of place where former sorority girls and fraternity boys go in an effort to stave off growing up—white girls with ponytails and guys with Michigan State sweatshirts and loud drunken voices; it's exactly what you think. Bill had been out with some friends of his, and, after listening to him obsess about this girl for three days, they finally goaded him into putting an ad in the personals to find her. The buck had thus been passed to me.

"Does this ever work?" he whined, and I told him yes. Yes. Well, sometimes. Maybe. It depends. I told him not to think about that, and to concentrate on the task at hand. He needed to tell me everything, every little thing he could remember about this woman, whom it turns out he had a somewhat hard time recalling. He'd been drinking, and it had been pretty late in the evening when he saw her and fell thunderstruck.

"So, what did she look like?"

"A goddess," he told me. "She had beautiful eyes."

"What color?" I asked.

"Oh, black," he answered. "I mean, uh, it was too dark to tell. But she had the most beautiful, dark, mysterious eyes. She smiled with her eyes."

You know, it's not always pleasant when people are poetic. She had black, beady, dopey, drunk-off-her-ass eyes. Just admit it. Hopefully she was sober enough to remember meeting him.

"Did you tell her your name?" I asked. "Did you talk about anything?"

"Uh, we didn't talk," he said shyly. "She wouldn't know my name. I didn't say anything to her."

"Well, did you *do* anything that would make her remember you?" I asked. "Like buy her a drink, or vomit on her, or pass out at her feet?"

"No!" he said. "Really, I wasn't that drunk, I swear. I just sort of stood next to her."

"You stood next to her?"

"Yeah. Sort of. It was really crowded, you know what Gamekeepers is like on a Saturday, and I would kind of move next to her and her friends, and then they would move, and I'd go get a beer and try to get close again, but I don't think she even noticed me."

"I know how it is," I told him. "You want to get closer, but the restraining order says two hundred fifty feet—what can you do?" This was met with a pained silence. "Sorry—just kidding. I'll try and behave. Okay. Can you give me a little bit more to go on here? Anything that might make her recognize who you were, who you are?"

"Uh . . . I was wearing my Michigan State sweatshirt that night."

How original.

"And jeans. And a baseball cap."

It's not that I'm heartless. This is a big cold city in a big nasty world, and finding the right person is difficult but ultimately worth it—blah blah blah. Try seeing it from my point of view. It's a crapshoot, it's a one-in-a-million chance, and, despite my optimism, sometimes those odds leave me cold. Finding love, finding satisfaction, finding that person you fell in love with in a bar and then losing her and then having to find her all over again—it's hard for me to give encouragement when I know exactly what the likelihood of success really is.

So, for me, in these cases it has to be business. Just business. Bill needed a personal ad, just the ticket when you're looking for someone and you don't know how to find them, the modern equivalent of standing on your roof with a bullhorn. Sometimes it's really easy: "You had sex with me in an alley behind the liquor store on Polk Street at two A.M. last Wednesday, please call," or "I stole your coat from the Elbow Room last Friday, during the second set of that band from Seattle that you said sucked, let's get together"—no problem, no sweat. But some searches are harder, and it doesn't help when people try their best to avoid being noticed, as Bill had clearly done.

A couple of days later I was on the phone with a woman who'd written a personal looking for a smaller gentleman—we were debating whether or not she should use *runt* in her ad; she didn't know if *runt* would sound playful and funny or grossly inappropriate. It might send a bad message. She wasn't sure. I put her on hold to think about that while I took a second call.

"Hi, Mr. Beaumier, it's Bill," the man said. "Do you remember me? I called you the other day. Remember?" He wanted to thank me for all my help, but he had an additional request. He was wondering if it was okay—if there wasn't some kind of rule against it, that is—to have more than one ad in the paper at a time. "Because if there is, I don't have to," he said. "It probably won't work anyway. But I thought I'd ask."

It had happened again. He'd fallen in love that morning—*that very morning!*—on his way to work. He'd been riding the el, and right by the door was the most beautiful woman he'd ever seen. Since the last one, anyway.

She was blond and "fresh"—his word—and he'd watched her from the time she boarded the train at Belmont Avenue all the way down to the point where she exited at Washington. He knew what he needed this time—all the details that would help him find this girl, his dream girl. With a leaky pen in a lurching railcar, he'd written down the time, the date, what she was wearing, and what she was doing, all inside the cover of his perpetually half-finished copy of *The Da Vinci Code.* He even wrote down the number of the subway car they'd been riding in.

"Well, that's sexy," I told him.

"She was reading a paperback book, just standing there reading." He sighed. "She didn't even notice me, but she was beautiful."

"What was the book?" I asked. "Could you tell?"

"It was a John Grisham book," Bill said. "I could see his name on it."

"Could you see the title?"

Silence.

"The title was too small," Bill said. "I couldn't make it out."

Why didn't he just introduce himself to this woman? In Chicago, where I happen to live, everything on the el is fair game. My friend Jenny used to fake Tourette's syndrome every morning just to get a seat, and she still managed to get phone numbers and invitations to dinner. I once sat next to a woman on the train who held my hand all the way downtown—nine stops. She was a few years younger than me, I'd never seen her before nor have I since, we didn't speak or even look at each other; we just held hands until she got off at the Merchandise Mart after murmuring "Thank you." The train is the single best place to meet people in Chicago—if you read the personals, you'd think there's more lust and heavy petting going on in the buses and on subways of the city than in all its bars and bedrooms combined. Bill could've asked this woman what she was reading or where she was going; he could've even pretended to be a confused and lost tourist in need of directions.

"But the train was too crowded—and women find it really creepy when strange guys talk to them on the train, you know that. I didn't want to come across like that."

"But guys *are* like that," I said, irritated.

Bill spied another woman two weeks later, sitting two rows behind him at the movies—tan blouse, black slacks—with two guys who he thought might just be friends ("They looked gay, but you never know, one of them might've been her boyfriend or something"). About a month after that, Bill wrote an ad looking for a woman who drove a blue Honda; she'd been getting gas at the same time he was ("She was getting in her car just as I was driving in, and our eyes locked, I'm sure of it, but maybe she was late for work or something so she just drove away"). Once he placed three ads seeking three different women he'd seen on the same night, at the same place—none of whom he'd had the courage to approach.

Depending on your point of view, this was either very sweet, or incredibly creepy and sad. To me, it was now annoying. I can accept the bittersweet drama of it all, and it wasn't like Bill was the only inhibited, timid person placing an ad. Personal ads were created for shy people, but shy people are not fun to talk to. Or to be around. They have interesting stories, I'm sure they do, though it's damn near impossible to get them to speak. Shy people don't inspire jealousy or cruelty or lust or any fun emotion, just impatience. They go to parties and stand next to the food, they never talk to anybody and nobody talks to them, and they make you feel guilty if you're having a good time yourself. Everybody has moments of introverted silence, but most people have the good sense to get drunk and get through them. Shy people stick to iced tea with a twist of pity.

And I now thought Bill sounded like a big, whiny baby.

Shyness is a disease, and it can lead to more serious ailments. Writing a personal ad to find the woman you glimpsed in the lingerie department at Saks or the man you bumped into during an intermission at Lyric Opera can easily turn, in the blink of an eye, from a charming quest to the most passive-aggressive form of stalking imaginable. There was a woman who once placed ads for almost a year seeking a man named Sean who very apparently did not wish to be found. I watched her turn from gooey maple syrup into bitter vinegar, and it was frightening to see.

"You moved," she wrote in one of her last ads, "and your new phone number is unlisted, but all this silly nonsense with the police can't erase that wonderful evening we shared. Wasn't it magic? Don't you remember? I'm here, waiting for you to come to your senses!"

Mostly, when people place these I-saw-you-somewhere-or-another personals, they aren't looking for a particular person so much as they are trying to say something they didn't have the courage or smarts to articulate at the time:

> *CHICAGO KINGS SHOW, February 28 at Metro. To the girl unabashedly flirting with Chip Starlight—watch out! He has a tiny weenie! I know, I've seen it. I'll be looking for you at the March 7 show at Circuit.*

> *LOAN COMMITTEE, 8/21. Saw you across the table, but I'm new from the architectural department and have never been properly introduced. Maybe we can read some blueprints over a cappuccino? I'll bring my scale.*

> *IRIS FROM TINA'S PLACE: we met at the last session, practicing knots. I'm John, introduced myself to you just before I tied your wrists together, and then you tied mine. You said you*

were new to public play. I'd love to get to know you better.
Coffee? Dinner?

These ads are fun even if sometimes the people who write them are not. Read the personals and you'll think you're seeing everything that goes on in a city, the near hits and regrets of people failing to connect with each other yet trying anyway. It seems exciting, like a great big diary filled with gossip and tawdry sex and bad hangovers—who went to what concert over the weekend, what movies people are going to, and which restaurants are best for people watching. But the thing you come to notice after a while is the sound of regret that runs through the words—the opportunities missed, the introductions not made, the things left unsaid. Wouldn't you think a person would have had his fill of wistful, sepia-drenched sadness by this point?

"You think I'm a big loser," Bill told me.

"Not yet," I told him. "But close." I wasn't kidding. I had been sympathetic and I knew the guy was shy bordering on mousy, sure—but while he wasn't a loser now, he was headed in that direction. I just didn't understand why he couldn't just—just *do something*. Take action, make a move, throw out a line. What's the worst that could happen? Women weren't going to run from him; I'd seen him, and he was better-looking than what you usually see at bars like Gamekeepers or in the subway or driving next to you on the Kennedy on the way to work. He came in to meet me after threatening for weeks to do so, and Bill was handsome. And I told him so. It was awkward.

I don't mind meeting people who place personal ads, the ones I've spoken to only over the phone, but it's always awkward. I know the whole point of what I do is to get people to meet each other, but I never understand why people who place personal ads feel the need to meet me. It's just my job. I never know what to say, so I just listen.

"I don't know what to do," he told me. "I've taken improv courses and gone to Toastmasters and all sorts of public-speaking classes and—and *look at me*! I can't even make eye contact with a girl, let alone speak to her." He was quiet for a moment, and then he let out a long sigh. I thought he might start crying, and I was getting ready to run. "You can't imagine," he said, "what it's like."

Actually, I could. Standing there awkwardly, across from him at the long service desk, I knew all about not knowing what to say.

So I didn't know what to say, and Bill didn't know what to say, but we both just kept standing there, each of us looking down at the counter. And I don't know why the idea popped into my head—guilt? too much coffee?—but I told him that maybe I could help him.

"Come back tomorrow," I told him. And then I went and started the letter; it didn't take long to write. Written words are easy. Written words are great things.

The next afternoon, I told him, "There are a lot of different ways that a nice fellow like you can meet an eligible young lady. And you are a nice fellow, Bill, a good guy. And you deserve a good woman. What you need, I think, is an intermediary, someone who can vouch for your intentions and all your good traits. Since I can't be with you all the time to do it, and since I'm probably more awkward and introverted than you are, I thought this might do the trick."

And this is what I wrote:

To Whom It May Concern:

My name is Mike Beaumier; I run the personal-ads department at a weekly newspaper here in Chicago. One section of the personals is dedicated exclusively to people who've crossed paths but didn't quite meet. You might have heard of it, or maybe not.

Anyway, the guy who handed you this note is named Bill.

I've come to know Bill very well. In many ways, he reminds me of my father—quiet, decent, someone who probably falls under the radar for most people. He neither drinks nor smokes, he's close to his parents and his siblings, he has a job, a home, a car, and someplace to be in the morning, and many friends who, like me, think highly of him. Once you get to know the guy, you'll wonder why nobody's snapped him up yet. I often do, and romance is my business.

No, he's not gay.

Business is business, I always say, but sometimes it's not. Which is why I'm writing this letter. Bill is very shy. Actually, that doesn't even come close to describing the situation. Bill is, apparently, almost terrified to speak. I'm not sure why; he's very smart and really funny. Perhaps he has an over-developed sense of reserve and propriety; maybe he was too aggressively toilet-trained as a child. It could be a chemical thing. Who knows? Or maybe he's a little too self-conscious for his own damn good.

I'm asking you—someone I do not know—to please, please, PLEASE save us all a lot of trouble and let this man buy you a cup of coffee. Because if you don't, Bill is just going to put another ad in the paper, and I will once more have to give him another lecture about having the courage to approach interesting women. And I'm quite sure you're an interesting woman because, while Bill is pathologically shy, he's nobody's fool.

If Bill doesn't give you his phone number, I will. Please feel free to call me at my office number listed below.

Sincerely,

Mike Beaumier

Personals Editor

Bill lowered his head, too surprised and sheepish to meet my gaze.

"You don't need to say anything," I told him, which was probably the nicest thing Bill could hear. "Make copies of this," I said. "I wrote only one, and I don't want you coming back here every five minutes needing a new one. In fact, don't come back here again. Ever. I expect to hear about you from some nice girls, but I don't want to hear it from you."

I shook Bill's hand and went back to my office. I never did hear from him again, but I didn't forget about him. Every time I ride the train to work, I look at all the people around me. The woman in green with light brown hair, putting on her makeup with a small pink mirrored compact. The older man standing in the doorway, amazingly keeping his balance while doing the *New York Times* crossword puzzle. The pretty but no-nonsense Philippine woman, her sons spilling out of their seats into the aisle, straightening out their clothes and zipping backpacks, her boys excited and talking loudly above the din of the el. Would they recognize themselves if someone wrote an ad? There you were. I knew you in a heartbeat. It's you I've been looking for all along, if only you could see it.

A few months later I came to work, and a call was waiting for me.

"She's been on hold for ten minutes," Dorie, the receptionist, told me. "She didn't want your voice mail. She wanted to speak to you live."

"Hello, is this Mike?" the woman said. She sounded guardedly amused, and a little bewildered—is that what *bemused* means? "The Mike who runs the personals? You don't know me, my name is Angie, and, well, I have a few questions to ask you about a fellow named Bill . . ."

NOT A GREAT ladies man, but a man meant for one great
lady. SWM 48, healthy, in good shape, dapper, intelligent,
well-read (Tennyson rules!), seeks soft heart and solid head for
wine, dine, and all that's fine. Meet me for a drink, and we'll
take it from there!

"Hello—Roger? Are you Roger? Goodness, I hope you haven't been waiting long, the weather, and the traffic—please, don't get up. I'm so sorry I'm late. I'm Gladys."

Please don't be Roger. Please don't be Roger. Please, please,
please. God, if you're up there, strike me dead right now. If
you're listening, send a lightning bolt straight to my heart and
blow me up into a million pieces, just don't make me have to
sit here with this—this—

"Oh, yes, I recognized you immediately—you're just how you described yourself in your ad, absolutely. 'Dapper' is just the right word for you, absolutely dapper, absolutely. I've always thought bow ties were so charming, terribly chic, though you hardly ever see a man wearing one anymore. Well, let's see. What's that you're drinking, Roger? Oh, that sounds lovely, I'll have one of those."

Well, this is just great. This is just wonderful. Here I am, having a drink with Pee-Wee Herman. Lovely. I'm on a blind date with a penguin—a short, bald, middle-aged penguin.

I should have asked how tall he was. I could just kick myself. He didn't say how tall he was in his ad, and that should've clued me in. When a man doesn't say how tall he is, he's just telling you how tall he isn't. It must hurt his neck having to look up to tie his shoes. Maybe the waiter can bring him a phone book to sit on.

I will kill Caroline. I will absolutely kill her. "Call him," she said. "He sounds nice," she said. Caroline and her big ideas. "I've met so many nice men through the personals, you should really give it a try"—well, I'm sure you're having a big laugh now, aren't you, Caroline? Just rocking with laughter, I'm sure. No wonder everyone in the marketing department thinks you're such a bitch. Caroline the bitch, that's what they say when your back is turned, did you know that? I've been your only friend, I'm the only one who's ever stuck up for you. Well, not anymore. You're dead to me, Caroline. Dead.

"My! That's a strong drink! No, no, it's delicious, though it burns a little bit. Goodness, I just—What? Bald? Why, I hadn't even noticed. It looks so becoming on you, it suits you perfectly—you have just the right shape head for no hair. Honestly, I thought you shaved it on purpose. Some men do that, and I was sure you were one of them."

Did I notice? Did I notice? My God, I was almost blinded when I walked in here. I can see my reflection, that's how bald we're talking—I wish he'd just lean in a little closer, so I could touch up my lipstick. I've never seen anyone so bald in my life. It must be nice that people can see you from space.

I'm never letting Caroline answer another personal ad for me, not for as long as I live. Never, never, never.

"Another one? Well, sure, why not? It's Friday after all, let's let our hair down—oh, I'm sorry. No, please, let me get this round. This one's on me. Okay, you can get the next one, then."

Caroline the whore. Yes, that's what they'll all be calling you Monday morning after I'm through with you. Whore slut whore! Is this funny to you? Is this how you get your jollies? "He sounds so cute—if you don't go out with him, I will. He's a real catch, I bet"—well, that's exactly the attitude I'd expect from you, Caroline. He's a catch, all right. You could catch him in one hand.

And just look at this pathetic little man. Poor what's-his-name. He looks so forlorn, with his little bow tie and his bald little head glowing like the moon hanging in the sky. My name—Gladys—is practically poetic! What a shame he's

bald and short and has a name like—Rodney? Roger. Life
can be so cruel. Cruel and short. And bald.

"Oh, I think it's lovely. This is an absolutely lovely place.
Absolutely! Though it is getting a little warm in here. It's warm, but it's
friendly. Do you come here often? After school? Are you a teacher?
Oh, a principal—well, that is something, isn't it? Yes, I'd need to
unwind too, if I were an elementary school principal. Not an easy job,
I'm sure, but it must be so fulfilling. The children truly are our future,
aren't they? You must just adore children. Oh. I see. Well. That must
make things hard."

At least you don't have to work with Caroline the bitch, the
whore, the warthog from hell—"Gladys, you should get out
more," she says. "Gladys, try putting on a little lipstick," she
says. "Gladys, I think you and this little bald penguin would
be perfect for each other." Rot in hell, Caroline.

I suppose it's not her fault. She tries her best, I know—and
she was right about meeting in public, somewhere dark and
far from the office. "If he's horrible, at least nobody will see
you—and if he's really bad, just say you're going to the
women's room and then slip out the front door." Caroline can
be smart. She really can be. I guess being raised by wolves has
its advantages.

And Rodney's not so bad. Rodney? Robert? Roger. It's
Roger, right? He's kind of cute, sort of. He's not so bad. I could

> *just pick him up and put him in my pocket. And a man who*
> *hates children can't be all bad, I guess.*

"Me? I work in auto supplies—in sales, mufflers, mostly. Oh, yes, it is fascinating. They have these absolutely wonderful machines now to make mufflers. It's all done with water so there aren't any edges or seams, and the corners are rounded to cut back on wind resistance. You wouldn't think wind resistance would be important when it comes to mufflers, but it most certainly is. Absolutely! And I work with some wonderful people. My friend Caroline—well, she's just a boatload of fun, always getting me into trouble. She's the salt of the earth. Really, she's my very best friend in the whole world. I don't know what I'd do without her."

> *Caroline was right—men just love it when a woman talks*
> *about cars. She was absolutely right. I have him eating out of*
> *the palm of my hand. Look at him there, with his chin on the*
> *table. He thinks I'm charming and wonderful. I am charm-*
> *ing and wonderful. Though I wish it wasn't so hot in here. I*
> *hope my mascara isn't running. I hate it when that happens.*

"Another? Oh, yes, let's have another round! But just one more, Robert, I don't want to get tipsy. Roger. Have I been saying Robert all this time? No, I feel wonderful, really. Absolutely wonderful. Waiter, we'll have two more, but just tiny ones. Little teeny tiny, okay? Oh, dear. What's the matter? What's wrong? That's terrible! Oh, how awful! How dare those awful children call you that!

"Don't cry. Please don't cry, Rodney. Robert. Teeny Tiny. Oh, c'mon, I think it's a sweet nickname, really. I'm sure the children call you that out of love, pure love. I tell you what—let's go back to my place, let's get outa here, and we'll have us some more drinks at my place. No, not at all. Of course you are! I wouldn't say it if I didn't mean it. I tell my best friend, Caroline, that all the time, and she's the nicest, nicest person in the whole world."

SADDLE UP, MEN! Looking to start a men's group to talk about our issues, bond and reaffirm our innate masculinity. Familiarity with drums, chant therapy, and the book A Circle of Men *helpful. Hugging mandatory. No alcohol, swearing or smoking.*

When you're single, you have a lot of strange theories about what it takes to have a successful marriage. Never go to bed angry; say "I love you" each and every day; never fight in front of the children (if you have any); make nice with your mother-in-law; phone when you're running late; attend church regularly; hold hands at the movies; forsake all others; make home-cooked dinners; take separate vacations; have sex 2.8 times per week; brush and floss regularly; do the dishes; take out the trash without being asked twice; and, if at all possible, have your own bathrooms.

In my family, we were taught that the secret to a successful marriage, or a successful anything, is *stamina.* If you and your beloved can make it to the point where you're too tired to chase anyone else and too weak to kill each other, you will bask in your triumph and serve as a model to others. My parents are that perfect example—they've been married for something like 750 years, and in all that time they've had only one argument. One long, constant, never-ending argument that they are each dead set on winning—an unresolved disagreement over the number of children they actually have.

To be fair, my parents did have a lot of children, and after the first four or five it probably got hard to keep track. No one disputes that there are two girls, Anne and Katie, both of whom stood out because they were blond, beautiful, clear-skinned, and girls. Two isn't very many, and it took a long time for me to learn to say I had two sisters without the word *only* thrown in. Girls were not the problem. The trouble was, as it always is, with the boys.

"Six," our mother says.

"Seven," says Dad. And off they go again.

We are—in order—Jack, Anne, Pat, Mike, Matt, Casey, Colin, Katie, and Paul. Mom is Irish. Say the names really fast—*jackannepatmike-mattcaseycolinkatiepaul*—and it sounds like machine-gun fire. People ask if our parents planned on having so many children, or if it was something that just sort of happened. It's the stupidest question. I doubt my father turned to my mother on their wedding night and nonchalantly asked, "So whaddya say, honey—eight or nine?" But we certainly weren't an accident, either. We were more or less a habit.

The arrival of a new baby was a regular event. Bets placed on gender and due dates would have to be paid, sleeping arrangements would be rearranged, a crib would be set up, and a tearful toddler would be told that his or her status as "new baby" had been officially downgraded. By the time Mom was pregnant with her ninth child, these arrangements had become routine, no big deal; we were a well-oiled machine, ready for wails in the middle of the night and the top shelf of the refrigerator to be taken up by bottles of formula. We were ready the day we came home from school in May to find our mother absent and our grandmother announced that we had a brand-new baby brother. Yet another win for the boys. We all knew the drill—Mom and baby would be home in a few days, we'd each get a chance to hug her and hold him, and on we'd go with our lives, just with one more.

Until baby number nine. Nothing was said, not that first day, but the grimness of our grandmother's silence told us that something wasn't right, definitely wasn't right. Grandma said nothing, but Dad didn't come home that night, or the next day, or for many days after, and in our parents' absence a sickening tension grew. It was a shock when Dad reappeared, exhausted, unshaven, trying to hide the sadness in his eyes and failing. He called us to the long dinner table and sat in silence for a long minute, and when he spoke it was with a tone we'd only ever heard him use when addressing grown-ups. Mom was very sick, he told us. The baby was sick too. Things looked very bad. He didn't know what was going to happen. He was going to be at the hospital a lot, and Grandma was going to take care of us. We needed to be extra well-behaved, the older ones had to take care of the younger ones, no fighting, no complaining, no fires, let the dog's fur grow back for once. Be good. There was no *or else,* no threat of punishment or offer of reward. He wasn't asking.

Our grandmother, our mother's mother, was old-school Irish, with a predisposition toward tragedy, especially when she had a couple of gin and tonics in her, which was most afternoons. Usually she had them with my mother while they played cards before the Herculean task of making dinner, but without our mother's joking and teasing and general merriment to balance her out, our time with Grandma became like a funeral. Grandma had been made an Irish widow at a very young age, left with no resources and a twelve-year-old daughter to raise by herself, and though she tried to suppress it, her mood was always one of mourning, and she was never so good at anything as she was at hanging crepe. We loved her, and we knew she was doing her best, but we felt sorrier for ourselves than for her. Grandma morosely insisted that we comb our hair, keep our voices down, and use curious phrases like "please" and "thank you." Grandma thought that half of a sour grapefruit and a bowl of cold oatmeal was an acceptable alternative to Cap'n Crunch, and it seemed like our lives were losing an equal amount of color, flavor, and sweetness. Grandma declared that matches, scissors, knives, glue, duct tape, and the mallet used to tenderize meat were not toys, and that from here on out we had to make our beds. But the worst was no fighting. *No fighting.* Was she serious? Not even sucker punches?

"Are you sure you're *our* grandma?" my eight-year-old brother, Matt, asked.

Days turned into weeks, and weeks into months. We saw our father rarely, usually very late at night, long after the sun had gone down, when he'd return from the hospital. No one knew exactly what had happened, and no one was brave enough to ask, but we figured out the basics—the baby had come, something went wrong, and Mom had nearly died. Her recovery was slow and very lonely; she had never been away from us for more than a week at the most, and she was as needy for us as we were for her, but Dad was hesitant. She was just too sick at first, and when we were finally allowed to visit her in the hospital, we could go only in small groups, two or three of us at the most. We didn't need to be told to behave ourselves, and, despite being doped up, Mom found this unnerving.

"Why aren't you *fighting*?" she'd ask from her bed, and her impatient eye-rolling was not from any pain medication. "They aren't like this at home, I swear," she would assure the nurses. "Who are you people? Somebody *hit* someone already." But Dad would shake his head *no*, and we'd cower by the door, afraid to do or say anything that might upset her.

The baby was rarely mentioned. There had been rumors of life support, and of priests called for sacraments ranging from baptism through last rites, but it was a forbidden topic. None of us younger kids saw Paul, as they'd named him, until very late that summer, when he and Mom were finally well enough to come home—a deliberately low-key celebration, especially compared to the raucous introductions new babies had received in the past. No one tried to feed Paul candy or introduce him to the dog by putting them both in the playpen. We weren't very clear on what Dad meant by Paul's "special needs," and when we gathered around the crib to finally get a look at him, he hardly seemed like the cause of so much trouble. He looked like any baby, except for the terrible shakes that would suddenly overwhelm him, and how his eyes would roll back in his head. The seizures were constant and brutal, overtaking his tiny body several times a minute; had I been old enough to understand what was happening, I would not have been able to bear it.

Being children, we immediately nicknamed him "Shakes." We weren't allowed to hold him, but we tried to outdo one another in impersonating him, convulsing on the floor or falling furiously over each other, fluttering and rolling our eyes as Paul did. We all had nick-names in our family—Pat was "Bunny," Colin was "Kiki," I was called "Mouse"—but Grandma was horrified with Paul's label, and quickly put a stop to its use. We didn't understand. The worst was over, wasn't it? Why did everyone seem so sensitive, and so tired? But eventually even we could see that this baby required a great deal of care, more than most babies. His needs changed day by day, sometimes minute by minute. There was no set routine with Paul, as there is with most new-borns—he did not eat normally, did not sleep according to any set schedule, could not be left to himself, and the task of caring for him soon proved to be overwhelming.

In hindsight, it was probably crazy to think that Mom could take care of eight children and a very sick newborn after nearly dying her-self. More than the agony of everything else, of all they'd been through, probably the worst thing for our parents was the realization that they simply could not tend to this child themselves. He was with us for only a matter of weeks before the decision was made. I don't remember the day they took him away, or saying good-bye, but we did not see Paul again for almost two years.

A gloom settled over us after Paul was gone—not anxiety, not tragedy, either, but this odd, nagging feeling of incompleteness. Someone was supposed to be there, and he wasn't. Even though he was just an infant, Paul's absence was acute, a presence in itself, and it was especially hard on Mom. Occasionally she and Dad would disappear without a word, telling us later that they'd gone to the place where Paul was, an institution of some kind in a town nearby. Mom would just suddenly want to see him, sometimes on the spur of the moment, and Dad never said no. Afterward, when we asked, Dad would tell us that Paul was fine, but there were never really any details. He existed somewhere, vaguely, and anything else was just pain and hurt. Mom would usually go upstairs after these journeys, shut her bedroom door, close the curtains, and crawl into bed. We had hoped that surviving Paul would be enough for her, but we were wrong. She missed that kid.

When he finally died, two days before his second birthday, it was like a bad spell had been broken. There would be a funeral, and sadness, and a terrible sense of loss—but there would also be an ending, finally, instead of the in-between place where he and all the rest of us had lived for so long. Because we hadn't seen him since he was an infant, Paul had become, to us kids, less a person than a situation. All that changed at his wake.

"Come and see your brother," our mother told us, and led us into the little chapel.

The casket was a tiny thing; you could put your arm around it. I don't know why I expected to see a baby, but that wasn't what he was. His hair had grown in, dark and full, and his features had become more pronounced and solid. The nose, the shape of his mouth, his thick bushy eyebrows, a face so familiar because it was mine, the face I shared with all the boys gathered around me, peering into the tiny coffin. My brother Colin—now the youngest brother, once again, only six years old—simply could not keep his hands off Paul, holding his tiny hands and touching his face. I understood exactly what he was feeling, the shock and surprise of it. Suddenly, he seemed like our brother. Suddenly, he seemed like one of us.

Personally, I thought he looked like Pat—though from certain angles he seemed more like Casey. Matt said he was a dead ringer for Jack, and immediately regretted his choice of words. Pat said he looked like a combination of Colin crossed with me, except without braces, which I took to be an affront and said so. Pat told me to stop being a jerk in church, and Matt pointed out that we were in a funeral home, not a church, and added the word *butthead* for good measure. Then Anne shoved Matt and Matt shoved Anne back, and Katie—four years old and now armed with a brand-new word—screamed, *"Stop it, you buttheads!"* at the top of her little lungs. Mom either laughed until she cried or vice versa. Dad made us all sit down.

We buried Paul, and we cried, and Colin dug a little hole over the grave and put some of his tiny plastic dinosaurs in for Paul to have. And then we went home and fought our way into adulthood, breaking into food fights and putting firecrackers down one another's pants, pushing one another out of windows, and filling one another's socks with jelly. And it was hard not to notice that these epic battles were, more often than not, instigated by our mother, who never seemed happier than when surveying the devastation, a gin and tonic in one hand, a cigarette in the other, a smirk of utter satisfaction on her lips.

Mom would arm us with spray paint and fake IDs, and her preference was for the anarchy and chaos of life. She expected us to sneak out for midnight keggers and smoke the illicit cigarette; she was actually quite adamant about such adventures, because she knew what the alternative was. She'd been raised in a house engulfed in grief, and she refused to give herself or us up to it. But even so, there was always something unsettled in the background, the unspoken thing that hung over all of us. Nobody talked about Paul. His birthday went uncelebrated, and his life and death, while never explicitly denied, was a forbidden topic. We'd visit his grave, of course, but we all knew not to bring up that time, or mention his name, because none of us could bear the look of pain that would appear in our parents' eyes. We knew that sometimes they would go to the cemetery by themselves, and on the days when Mom was especially quiet, when she wouldn't encourage us to take a slug at one another or set fire to anything, we knew where she'd been. She and my father were Paul's most frequent visitors, and even years later, after all of us kids had grown up and moved out and begun families of our own, after they'd sold the house and left town themselves, they would drive for hours, sometimes on the spur of the moment, just to be there—a habit neither age nor time nor distance could break.

* * *

The living mean more than the dead, and the living go on and they forget. But sometimes the elements conspire to bring the past and the present together again, and the dead remind you of all they once were.

There was a winter of extraordinary snow, followed by a spring of heavy, incessant rain. Rivers rose, the waters came, and a terrible flood engulfed our old hometown. Half the city was under water—the bottom half. Unfortunately, the top half was still quite dry. No one knows how the fire started exactly, but it jumped from building to building, burning everything straight down until the fire met the water. When it was over, nearly everything was destroyed—except the cemetery.

Maybe it was because there was no longer any place for them to stay. Maybe it was because they didn't like driving so far for so long. Or maybe they just didn't want him to be there all alone, in the middle of nowhere, with no one to mow the grass or put flowers on his headstone, or remember who he was. But at some point, my parents hatched their little plan for Paul. They'd have him disinterred and moved to where they were now in upper Michigan, where they had gone to live—to be buried next to my grandmother.

The casket was flown as far as Wisconsin, where, for reasons that still remain somewhat murky, my parents decided they'd finish Paul's journey on their own. My father had gotten very specific measurements of Paul's casket—the length and width and weight, and he'd borrowed a pickup truck that would accommodate the task. But apparently, to the surprise of probably no one except my parents, the rules about moving a body tend to be rather strict. You can't just haul around a casket that's been stuck in the ground for more than twenty years; the casket itself has to go into a special container of its own—one that's clearly marked and labeled.

Dad did not think it was as funny as the shipping dispatcher did when the box proved to be too long to fit in the truck. He did not think it was funny when the box was strapped in using extension cords. And he certainly didn't think it was funny that he had to pull the truck over to the side of the highway every ten miles, and he and my mother would have to get out and push the massive box marked CAUTION: HUMAN REMAINS back into the truck as cars zipped past, the other drivers' necks snapping around at the sight of two old people and box of bones, their mouths hanging open, their eyes agog.

But Mom loved every moment. Burying a son once is tragic, but twice—well, that's a habit. She took great pleasure in calling each of her children after arriving home, letting us know that she and Dad were back from a long journey, that our father was exhausted from the drive, and that a box containing our beloved baby brother was currently sitting in their garage. There was an old, almost forgotten glee in her voice that we all noticed; she seemed to revel in our shock, and laughed at our perplexed horror. She'd never joked about Paul, never. And sure, the jokes were utterly tasteless and wholly inappropriate—but it was nice to see her old, wicked personality kick in. Suddenly, Paul wasn't off limits.

"They're getting creepy," my brother Matt said.

"Well, that's what happens when you get old," Colin said. "You never throw anything out."

"Remind me to be cremated," I told my brother Casey.

"It won't matter," Casey responded. "That'll just make you easier to cart around wherever they go."

"Paul's obviously their favorite," Pat said drily. "Of course, it's easy to love a kid that you don't have to always try to shut up." And there he was, Paul was back among us, one of us brothers at last. We didn't even know we had missed him—we didn't know we *could* miss him. Years of silence and confusion were replaced overnight with deeply inappropriate dead-baby jokes and everybody's favorite, sibling rivalry. Where, we wondered, would they be taking Paul next? Disneyland? We never got to go to Disneyland.

"You never took us anywhere!" we cried.

"How could we?" Mom told us. "You kids were always fighting."

But Mom was clearly the worst. She relished our gross-out humor and always managed to do one better. Not long after all this, she called each of her sons, one by one, to ask in her most serious and earnest voice if we'd ever had a, you know, "bad experience" with a priest when we were kids. This was in the middle of a terrible molestation scandal, and she told us that she absolutely, positively, wanted to know. One by one we assured her that nothing of the kind had ever happened, that our priests were good guys, that no one had tried anything, ever.

"Well, *shit,*" she told me. "That's what your brothers said. I must have raised the six *ugliest* boys on the face of the earth." And as she laughed and laughed, delighted that she'd gotten another one of us, Dad's voice piped up somewhere behind her, vaguely irritated at having to remind her, yet again.

"Seven!"

HOT KINKY SUPERFREAK wanted by attractive SWM, 30 years old, 6', 185#, brown/brown, college degree. I'm looking for a naughty SF, extremely fun and silly, likes dancing, pop culture and has a 70s-80s fashion sense.

Everybody who works here is in a band. The guys who deliver the newspapers have two or three rock bands, the receptionists are rappers and DJs, the maintenance guy is sometimes out on tour and the garbage piles up, and editorial is where old-school punk never dies. There are about six grunge bands involving various members of the classifieds department, emo has taken hold of the people who lay out the paper every week, and a girl in advertising has recently become besotted with a guy in a Mexican goth band called Los Tombres. You name it, at this newspaper they play it. Except for big band music. Nobody cares much for Bing Crosby or Dinah Shore or Dean Martin around here—or anywhere, for that matter—except me.

I like to think of this newspaper as a band—everyone has an instrument and an ego, but we're more or less forced to play together. The newspaper where I work takes up six floors of a building, each with its own particular life and character, each baffled at or odds with or just willfully oblivious of the others. The higher you go, the more important the people become, and at the very top, of course, are the owners and publisher. They're higher up because higher up is closer to God—from where they sit, they can look down on Him and all the rest of us.

It was not always so. Back in the day, when the owners first started the paper, they did everything—wrote stories, laid out pages, sold advertising, got drunk and slept around—and the paper was a daring and innovative thing, edgy and young. Every major city has at least one alternative weekly newspaper, providing a lively and hungry counterweight to the bland, boring, conservative, and stifling dailies. The owners published stories that other papers wouldn't touch or refused to see, and served an audience of readers that the daily papers didn't even know existed—smart, urban, vaguely disaffected, and hungry for something new.

It was an attractive alternative, not only to readers but also to advertisers, and the paper became, eventually, quite profitable. And what's true of any successful enterprise was true of the paper: success breeds management. Nowadays, it's widely assumed that the owners don't even read the paper; they just sort of keep an eye on it.

Beneath the layers of owners and managers is the advertising department. Ad sales people are easily identifiable, as they are the only ones in the building who dress well and shower regularly; they look as if they smell very clean, though I've never been close enough to one to know for sure. The advertising staff can't read, but they sure know how to count; they always reliably know precisely how many pages there are in this week's edition, and can endlessly quote circulation figures and distribution schedules. They are the only ones among us who could reasonably claim to have real jobs.

Next is the production department, the copy-and-pasters, the people who design the paper and lay out each page every week using a combination of computers, scissors, paste, and, occasionally, their own spit. They don't look terribly clean; they, in fact, look pretty grubby. Despite this, they are all very sexy. Production exists in its own little colorful, messy world—a place where outsiders are typically not welcome. Outsiders talk about words, stories, ads, and headlines, and Production only wants to talk about inches. Words are not so much concepts to be read and savored as they are objects to be arranged and rearranged, not unlike a jigsaw puzzle, until they finally achieve proper bold simplicity. Reading the paper would only get in the way.

Tucked away somewhere in the middle of the building, almost as an afterthought, is the editorial department. Editorial is where they keep the writers, critics, columnists, proofreaders, and a veritable smorgasbord of editors—junior editors, senior editors, managing editors, executive editors; one is hard-pressed to explain the distinctions among them, but suffice it to say these are people who are rabidly aware of where they appear on the masthead.

At normal newspapers, writers get respect, adoration, fame, and no money. Here, they just get no money. It's hard to be sympathetic. It's hard to work up any feeling for the editorial department other than an indifferent shrug, which is almost too cruel. Journalists everywhere like to think that people hate them—being hated, for a journalist, is almost as good as getting paid; it means someone's at least paying attention—but no one good enough to be hated stays here for long. The rest tend to go on and on, year in and year out, writing a lot without saying much. Goddamn them, and God help them.

Forced, unhappily, to share the bathrooms with the editorial staff above them, the classifieds department gets no respect, and demands none. It's just the classifieds department, after all. They take and type advertisements for apartment rentals, garage sales, job postings, and prayers to St. Jude, and aspire to nothing more than the end of the workday, after which they drink and grouse. No one has more direct contact with the people who actually read the newspaper, people who are often not terribly well-behaved. Despite this, they rarely lose their patience; they are simply not paid enough to take any of it seriously.

In the basement below them is the archive. Nobody actually works down there, that's just something they call it. It's where they throw old newspapers, and periodically there's a flood or a mouse or just no more room, so the papers are hauled out and recycled or sent someplace else. Maybe they go to newspaper hell, I don't know. I sit just above the archive, hidden away in a corner of the classifieds department, which should give you a pretty clear idea of where I'm located on the food chain. There's definitely a pecking order, and I'm at the bottom. Anything less and I wouldn't be in the building at all—which would make me the lowest of the low, the thing that gets less than no respect, something too terrifying to even contemplate: a freelance writer.

It might be my imagination, but most people in the building seem to steer clear of me. I am, after all, the guy who gets the weirdest phone calls, the strangest visitors, and the most disturbing mail. It was such a letter that brought one of the interns from editorial down to my office one morning; she arrived holding an envelope away from her body with two fingers, as if the contents included bloody bandages and used condoms.

"I think," she said, "that this is for you."

> Dear Sir or Madame Whoever You Are:
>
> I sent you an ad with a heading that I wanted in bold print titled, WANTED: WOMAN WITH VERY BIG FEET. I also wanted the entire headline in uppercase. I wrote the headline in bold print and then started the ad on the next line in regular ballpoint pen so that there could be no mistake of my intentions.
>
> Instead, you printed the ad (enclosed with this letter) with only half my headline in bold print. The part that mattered most importantly to me, VERY BIG FEET, was printed in regular font and in lowercase!
>
> I'm pissed off big time! The impact that I intended for the ad has been significantly diminished. I would like an extra week for free and if you're not willing to do that then give me an extra week at half price.
>
> Sincerely Pissed Off,
Pablo P.
>
> *P.S. Don't try to tell me that there wasn't enough room to bold print my entire heading.*
>
> *P.P.S. Be discreet when you respond to this letter.*

"Oh, that's just Pablo," I told her. "He finds something to complain about every week. I always know when it's open-toe-shoe season, thanks to Pablo." I smiled, but she didn't. "Don't worry. I'll take care of him."

"Freaks," she said, probably meaning both him and me, and she practically ran back upstairs to safety.

Guilt by association. What's worse—the freak show, or the guy who runs the freak show and obviously loves the freaks?

"Two things," Jeff announced at the door of my office. "Someone's at the front desk asking for you, and can you borrow me ten bucks?" Jeff types out personal ads once I've corrected the spelling or made edits, though most of the time I'm correcting or editing him. I tend to think of people in comparison to my brothers; Jeff has my brother Matt's laid-back charm plus my brother Colin's manic energy, divided by my brother Casey's belief in the inevitable power of good in the world. Jeff can be haughtily righteous and generously accepting at the same time, and he's never so serious that he can't laugh at something. Especially himself. And more especially me.

"I can *lend* you ten bucks," I corrected, handing him two fives. "Who's at the front desk?" I was expecting a woman who wanted to place an ad offering to donate one of her kidneys and a man who really, really, *really* needed to talk about what kind of woman he was looking for, and I wanted to be prepared.

"What's-her-name, that mousy chick who always asks for you," Jeff said. "The whore."

"*Adult service provider,* jeez."

"Yeah, yeah, whatever," Jeff said, and smirked.

We are never supposed to admit that we know what these ads are about. This is the rule at every newspaper. As far as we know, these are just caring women who are paid to hold the hands of elderly gentlemen at the movies, who listen to their boring stories and nod sympathetically when they complain about their wives and children. But this particular woman has an ad that always begins with the words *fast* and *loose*.

I have no idea what her name is, but I've seen her just about every week for the past three years. And every week it's the same story.

"I'm supposed to pay for an *ad*?" she told me—though it sounds like a question. Everything she says rises up a little at the end, which makes her sound all the more calculated in her disingenuousness. "They gave me this *money*? I don't know what it's *for*?" She's probably twenty-five or so, though she looks quite a bit older. I normally don't deal with the prostitutes or their pimps—my job is to deal with the people who offer or want sex for free—but she always asks for me. She knows I'm willing to believe, regardless of evidence to the contrary, that she's just helping some unfortunate prostitute friend of hers, out of the goodness of her heart.

Most of what I do is take people at their word, even when I know they aren't quite telling the truth—at that point it becomes more about the goodness of my heart than theirs, but I figure they aren't so much lying to me as they are in denial themselves. It's like the music makers who surround me; many of them might be hugely talented, just waiting to be discovered and whisked away to renown and riches—but somehow I suspect this might not actually be the case. In all the years I've worked at the paper, I've never actually gone to hear anyone's band, not once. Little postcards announcing someone's gig at a bar I've never heard of will show up on my desk, and I get e-mail messages promising no cover charge if I tell the doorman who I am—but still, I don't go. I don't know much about music, but I suspect I might know enough to realize that I hate what I'm hearing.

I took the mousy nonprostitute's money and wished her well, and she looked relieved that this embarrassing interaction was over for another week. Jeff and Andy were sitting in my office when I got back.

"Me and sucker here are going outside to smoke," Andy announced. "Do you have any smokes we can bum off you?" Andy is the other personals typist; he's about the same height and build as Jeff—tall and scrawny-thin, a sort of asexual, quintessential twenty-something look, though Andy is quietly heterosexual and Jeff is loudly not. Andy also wears a small silver hoop on his right eyebrow, and he's neither as vulgar nor as obnoxious as Jeff—which, when I think about it, doesn't require much effort. Other than these minor differences, they are virtually identical and often inseparable.

Andy and Jeff have lately been calling each other "sucker," for reasons I couldn't explain because I don't know, or care. Andy, in case you're wondering, seems to have my brother Jack's ribald sense of humor combined with my brother Patrick's naked ambitiousness. Which doesn't explains anything, either.

Jeff hates Andy's girlfriend. Andy hates Jeff's boyfriend. They both think the other can do better, and never miss an opportunity to say so. *Sucker!* While Jeff is content to see whatever the future holds for him, Andy wants to be on the radio—he's typing personals while interning at a radio station, and is trying to produce his own show. He brings me

CDs and tapes every so often, and while I'm sure they're very good, I don't have anything to play them on.

The only place to smoke is outside in front of the building, which is littered with dozens of cigarette butts despite the admonishments from management. You can tell who's been having a bad day by observing the type, quantity, and relative freshness of discarded smokes— everyone in the production department smokes Merits, writers and editors smoke Parliaments, while the classified department is apparently addicted solely to Camel Lights. Delivery drivers, a breed unto themselves, roll their own. I'm apparently the only person in the company who smokes Marlboro Lights, which Jeff and Andy begrudgingly accept when I follow them outside for a puff, only because they have no other option.

"At least they're not menthol," Jeff groused.

"Did you listen to my tape?" Andy asked, and groaned when I told him I hadn't. Nearby, a group of editors and proofreaders were smoking in their own little group, ignoring us while we ignored them.

We talked mostly about the folks who were placing personal ads, and often these conversations are not entirely kind. I've noticed lately a large number of personal ads from men who like to get punched, which, like all fetishes, is fascinating and hilarious. How exactly do you come to the realization that getting punched is sexy? Given that I see all the ads that run in the personals, I tend to dismiss these things as fads—before punching, it was spitting; before that, everyone was into spanking. Next year, it will be something different. My money is on slapping, through Jeff is sure that stomping is poised for a comeback. But right now, punching is the new black.

Our latest strangeness involves two suburban women Jeff has dubbed the Dueling Estelles. Every week for the past three months, I hear about one, and I hear from the other. They are both older Jewish ladies from the suburbs, and they make my life hell. The first Estelle is a bit of a mystery; I've never talked to her, but I've heard from a lot of her dates. She insists that her gentlemen take her out to dinner and pick up the check, and then she vanishes, never to be heard from again. She's left a trail of broken hearts and empty wallets in her wake.

"She's a cruel wench," said Andy.

"No, she's not, sucker," Jeff countered. "She's just full, that's all—she couldn't eat another bite."

"You pays your money," I said, flicking my cigarette butt in the street, "and you takes your chances. I wonder who she is—I've called her three times, and she doesn't even call *me* back. At the rate she's going, she's going to run out of good men and good restaurants. She'll be lucky to get drive-through at McDonald's."

As luck would have it, the other Estelle was waiting on hold when we came back inside.

"*Miii*-chael! It's Estelle! Estelle from *High*-land Park!" Estelle is a sixty-something-or-other-year-old from the suburbs, and she is a woman head over heels in love with the sound of her own voice. I've never met her in person, but I can imagine her on the other end of the line, animated like a cartoon character, rolling her eyes, savoring the deliciousness of her every utterance.

I put Estelle on hold and got some coffee. I then checked my mail. I contemplated cleaning the lint from behind my computer monitor or studying Sanskrit, but seeing that she was still waiting on hold, and knowing that she wouldn't hang up until she said whatever she was calling to say, I reluctantly picked up the phone.

"So, *Mi*-chael," she said, "I don't know if I've *ever* mentioned this, but I have *quite* the reputation as a successful matchmaker *myself.*"

She has mentioned this probably close to a dozen times. She never fails to mention this. That she's already married, and has been for a long, long time, has no bearing on any part of our conversations whatsoever. She knows all about love. You needn't even bother to ask. She'll tell you. All you can do is try to get her off subject.

"How's the ad working out for you?" I asked. "Have you met any nice guys?"

"Freaks!" she shrieked. The second, though probably not the last, time I would hear that word today. "It's a *freak show* out there! All these men think of nothing but *sex!* Just because a woman—a *lady*—is married and places an ad looking for a man for a discreet relationship . . ."

"Estelle?" I interrupted. "I'm sorry, you know how much I love hearing from you, but I've got a couple of calls waiting." It's hard to fake earnestness, but she doesn't seem to notice one way or the other. "I feel terrible about these awful, terrible men—is there anything I can do?"

"Oh, I suppose I just have to *weed* them out. But you're *such* a *nice*—"

"Okay-then-delightful-chatting-with-you-as-always-buh-bye-now." And I hung up.

*   *   *

People are shocked to find out that I have this much contact with the advertisers. I'm sometimes shocked too. I don't talk to all of them, of course—there are dozens of new people placing ads every day, several hundred every week, and most of them never realize that there's actually a real live person behind the curtain, correcting their spelling and fixing their grammar and watching their every move. This is probably for the best. Jeff and Andy make a daily habit of ripping apart each other's love lives, but I tend to be more sympathetic—except when the advertisers cannot seem to leave me alone, like Estelle. They ask advice on what to wear on dates, the best places to go for dinner, what movies they should see. They tell me about their worst dates, their worst fears, and their worst habits. As with most people, they're sometimes delightful, and sometimes they're just annoying. Mostly, they're exhausting.

There are stacks and stacks of their ads in my office—the lovelorn, love-starved, and loveless; the fetishists, sickos, cheaters, and liars. I haven't met most of them, I probably wouldn't recognize them if I did, but still, I know them. They're the ones who have slowly but irresistibly come to the realization that they can find love and/or sexual satisfaction, or they can keep their dignity—but usually not both. So I spend my days with the Dueling Estelles, the Denial Whore, the Incredibly Middle-aged Virgin Lady, and the One-Armed Couple Looking for a Three-Way (Jeff calls them "Mr. and Mrs. Stumpy"). I understand them; so do Jeff and Andy, and so does anyone who's ever been paid next to nothing to do something they love. You either watch the freak show, or you're in it.

[7] *Certain Names Have Been Changed*

*MEN ALL KNOW not to buy the cow when you can get the
milk for free. Well, why marry a pig when all you want is a
link? The pork must be tender and include special seasonings.
No bull for this SPF 23 who's searching for a SM 28–35.*

Most of us guard our privacy for a very good reason: shame. If people
knew what we were really like, if they had any idea as to our very true
natures, it's doubtful we could ever raise our heads in decent company again. Shame is a truly wonderful thing, not only because it
presupposes that such a thing as "decent company" actually exists,
but also because it's the only thing that keeps total strangers from
eagerly divulging the most filthy intimate details of their most depraved
fantasies.

That's the way it's supposed to work, anyhow. Not here. Around
here, people lose their inhibitions, speak frankly and share openly. In
the personals, there is no such thing as shame.

And believe me, that's a real shame.

Dear Mistress:

I'm a submissive white male who likes to be pinched. My last mistress died and I am currently in the market for a new one. Can be your houseboy, personal slave, into either forced oral to anal. To me also. In to crossdressing if commanded. Also into leather and lingerie.

Also if commanded can be humiliated if you command.

Also into full body massages. Also love to be abused any way you want while I service you at your command. Tie me up if wished. Also can be your whipping boy. Also will bathe you, dress you, whatever you command. Also looking for any SM/BD clubs or organizations where we can get together.

> Thank you,
> (possible) Mistress,
> John Smith

It's amazing the things people will tell you, the eager little tales they simply have to share, the forbidden scenarios they've played over and over in their heads, now given the opportunity to spill out of their mouths. I like to think that I inspire this candor, that there's something special about me that somehow compels otherwise reticent people to confess their bed-wetting fetishes and rape fantasies. I'd like to think I have that kind of power, but in truth, I'm just a guy who's lost the ability to be appalled.

Everyone knows this. My blasé attitude, my quiet sighs of boredom, the eye-rolling—it's obvious at this point. Everyone also recognizes that even if I were the kind of fellow who got all excited and squeamish over dirty filthy sexy stuff, there wouldn't be a lot I could do about it anyway. The advertisers and I understand there is, by the nature of our dealings, an implied trust that exists between us, an unwritten, nonverbal contract, an assumption. I will keep your secret. I won't judge. I'll help you find a woman who'll let you rub balloons all over her body, or a man who thinks nothing is hotter than eating gummy bears out of your butt. Fine. This is my job, I'm just doing my job, and my job is to keep my mouth shut. Right?

Right.

> Dear Ad Person:
> This is how you all must improve your personals. You must put the ladies who are lesbian in there with there name, age, zip code, city and state and don't forget there address also. I must see all this for myself.
>
> Sincerely,
John Smith

> P.S. Don't forget about me at all.

There is no spellcheck, no filter, no subtlety, no euphemistic nuance—just the low, snarling growl of physical need put forward in the most graphic, and least attractive, terms possible. People want me to know the terrible tawdry things they've done, do, and want to do again; they describe themselves and their partners and their acts of coupling in excruciatingly moist detail, and show no hesitation in sharing things with me that they would probably not tell their doctors. And yet, four times out of five, they will not tell me their real names.

"I don't want you to know who I *am*," they always say. I hear this from people who send me pictures of themselves naked, people who describe their sexual habits and histories in exhaustive, and exhausting, detail—people who, when you come right down to it, have nothing left to hide. They can let it all hang out, except for what people call them.

Dear Nice Lady:

Oh my gosh! When I saw your ad, my heart stopped. My whole world stopped. My first thought was, God—please, please, please, let her choose me. You see, I'm a single white male who just so happens to be everything you are looking for in a man! Thoughts of being with you consume my waking thoughts. It has been a life-long dream of mine to be your man, so much that I am actually answering your personal ad from the newspaper! I cannot wait to meet you!

I can't implore enough on you of my sincere desire to be your love and companion for all time. My commitment to you would be 100 percent.

> Hoping to be your
> future husband,
> I Love You,
> I Mean It,
> John Smith

Okay. Sometimes we do things that we're embarrassed about later. We've all done things that we regret. Sure, some of us have been on the covers of bondage magazines, and some of us have had sex in garbage bins behind bars, while handcuffed—it happens. The world might not understand, but I do. I'm here to help. But I can't do anything if I don't know who you are.

> Dear Editor:
>
> Help! I gave the wrong phone number in response to a personal advertisement in last week's edition of the paper ("Big Hairy Daddy"). I foolishly gave my kids' (and ex-wife's) home telephone number. Please tell her to use my work number instead. I'd much appreciate it.
>
> > Thanks,
> >
> > John Smith

There are so many places in life where we wallow in anonymity, unseen and unheard. Those moments we get where we can say who we are, and what we want—even if it's to be tied up by two guys in sweatpants with no underwear, because that's your thing—well, even though those moments aren't brief and few enough for me doesn't mean they shouldn't be important to you. Stand up and say your name, I'm listening and I promise to try my best not to laugh.

> To Whom It May Concern:
>
> I would like to express my displeasure and *outrage* over the treatment I received from a date I met through your personals section.

My date, Mr. John Smith, placed a personal ad last June in which he portrayed himself as a great catch that I couldn't resist responding to. He finally got around to calling me and we agreed to meet for drinks and dinner. I found him to be rude and insensitive, and not at all like he portrayed himself in the ad. First of all, when he arrived he was clearly intoxicated. Second, he was DIVORCED, even though in his ad he said he was a SWM (single white male). DIVORCED is not SINGLE!

Within five minutes he was asking me questions about sex that I found to be extremely offensive. I mean, this is the first meeting and I'm being asked what my favorite sexual position was, and whether I did threesomes and if I was into pinching. All he talked about was pinching. When I said I didn't think it was appropriate for him to talk this way, he said, "Women are always telling me that." Then why does he do it? He then revealed that he had all kinds of problems with women, including an earlier arrest for stalking which he claimed to be a misunderstanding. He says he wasn't in jail that long. I asked him how he ended up in jail if it was all just a misunderstanding. He said that all women are crazy. He seems like one of the characters that appear on the Jerry Springer show.

If this is what he revealed to me on the first date, I wonder—what else is he concealing? How many other crimes has he committed? How many other times has he been in jail? How many other ex-wives does he have? Does he have kids he neglects to mention? Does he even have a job? Does he really live where he says he lives? Now that I think about it, is his name even real?

To top it all off, he made me pay for half of dinner and then asked me if I wanted to go with him to another bar. After all this, did he think I wanted to spend more time with him? I'm glad I had something else planned. As I was getting in my cab he said, "We'll have to do this again, I'll call you." Sure. When hell freezes over. And he hasn't even called.

You people need to do something to screen out the perverts, drunks and men who are abusive towards women. I don't know what you do to screen the men, but whatever it is, it clearly isn't working. How many other women is he meeting through your ads?

Something needs to be *done*. We don't need sex-crazed jerks like John Smith running around and harassing innocent women like me.

Sincerely,

Jane Doe

45 YEAR OLD VIRGIN seeking the one. I'm attractive and fun to be with, and have dated a lot. I just haven't found the one. I'm looking for a man who doesn't masturbate, believes in celibacy before marriage, is nonsmoking, atheistic or at least agnostic, is lean and respects his body. I'm gentle, assertive and demand respect.

My very first day on the job, I was told about a woman who'd worked in the personals until she got so freaked out that she finally snapped. The madness began, as it so often happens, in the ladies' room. People noticed she was spending a lot of time in there, washing her hands, and it wasn't long before she began scrubbing her face with equal frequency and gusto, until her cheeks matched the bright, sad pink of her fingers. It was the mail that set her off. Every day there were letters from desperate singles, cheating spouses, sexual compulsives, prison inmates, people into the most bizarre and disgusting fetishes. Had any of them washed their hands? Had they licked the envelopes?

She stopped answering her phone. The handset was surely a witches' brew of germs and bacteria, and the perverts on the other end of the wire made her sick enough. Everything, everywhere, was dirty. She avoided doorknobs, handrails, and, ultimately, people. Another lost cause, they all said, and they sadly shook their heads. Another decent, earnest young person who arrived bright-eyed and hopeful, and left crazy and smelling of Lysol. She hadn't, apparently, been the first. Inevitably, people who work in the personals become angry and disillusioned—is this what love is? Cheap lies, half-truths, delusion, deception, and fraud? No wonder people leave feeling unclean; no detergent can get out those really deep stains. No one remembers if she left or was finally asked to leave, but last anyone heard, she was going to graduate school at Arizona State. To get an MFA.

Yep. It's a sad story.

"It sure is," the woman across the counter from me replied. "But I still don't get why I gotta tell you my real name."

I'd been trying for ten minutes to convince her that she could trust me. I'd gone from amiable to enchanting and landed at charismatic, which is no easy thing when you've got a four-foot-high counter standing between you and your audience. I'd regaled her with clever stories and charming anecdotes about my bosses and my predecessors, and I was ready to trot out my employees to do card tricks, if necessary. I entertained her, and I assured her. I told her she would not be put on some desperate-singles mailing list. I told her no salesmen would call. I told her that the newspaper kept everything strictly private, and that we stopped selling our more attractive advertisers off as sex slaves to overseas drug cartels months ago. What I wanted to tell her, really, was that she didn't need to worry. She really wasn't that unique or special, there were going to be three or four more just like her today, and I never remember names anyway. But I figured that would be a little too honest.

She looked to be about fifty years old, though she claimed in her ad to be in her late thirties; I couldn't tell if the discrepancy was the product of a lie or a hard-knock life. There was the hint of a rumor of what very well may have once been beauty in her face, but all that remained was the expression of someone who'd gone on too many bad dates, someone too often called upon to be a good sport. She claimed to be a bubbly blonde, but she looked big and bulbous, and her hair was graying at the roots, frizzy, and unkempt. She was more than a little loud, which she chose to characterize as "earthy." This was the first time she'd ever written a personal ad, I could tell. I hadn't seen her before, there wasn't a single word of truth in what she'd written, and— most obvious of all—she had the look on her face. The *my-God-it's actually-come-to-this* look.

And because of this, Bubbly Earthy refused to tell me her name or address.

"Listen," I told her. "People come in here all the time placing personals with fake names. John Smith, Jane Doe, Dick Johnson, Anita Mann. Dumb names. *Stupid* names. I had six Bridget Joneses going for a while there; I thought I was going to lose my mind. And still, if a week goes by when I don't have at least one Tyler Durden, I get worried."

Her eyes were wide and blank.

"Fight Club," I explained. "They made it into a movie. A chick flick for guys."

"But what happens to all my information when you finally flip out like what's-her-name?" she wanted to know. "What do you want it for? Who's gonna see it?"

I've learned not to say "Trust me" to people who've been on a lot of really bad dates. They've heard those words before, and it immediately puts them on edge. But I shouldn't have to say it, anyway—the only person with access to names and addresses is me, and giving such information out to strangers is, I suspect, one of those things that would get my ass fired. She could trust me with her name, and that I would tell no one of her fondness for Meg Ryan movies and long walks on the beach; the special secret of her love of ethnic foods and thrift-store shopping would die with me. The real question, when you think about it, was if I could trust *her*. After all, I was the one who knew she was lying about having an "obsession" with Monday night football. Was my life in danger? Did I know too much? After all, she knew what I looked like—and where I worked.

"So you get to meet everybody in the personals, huh?" she asked. Apparently we were going to talk about *me* for a while.

"Some of them," I told her.

"Any hotties?" she asked.

"Eh. A few. Besides *you*, of course." I am nothing if not all charm.

"It must be great to work here," she said. "You must meet a lot of girls. I'm sure a cute guy like you is pretty popular."

"I'm too old to be cute," I told her. "The cutoff for cute is like twenty-four years old. I'm way past cute. Thank God."

She leaned in close to the counter. "What's your name?"

"I'll tell you mine if you tell me yours," I smirked.

I know, I know—I shouldn't flirt. Around here, flirting is danger-ous, because you never know what you're getting yourself into. Not everyone who places a personal ad is looking for love. Yes, a lot of people are seeking a gooey, gauzy, happily ended kind of romance, but there are other people whose needs are of more, uh, short term. Actu-ally, I've always found it easier to deal with the sex people than the love people; their needs are more direct, more immediate. When I was hired to work in the personals, I was told about the weird sex stuff—I was going to see things I'd never seen before, dirty, twisted things from seemingly normal people who, in their private hours, were anything but. The man who wanted to ride another man around like a horse, with boots and saddles and spurs and everything. The woman search-ing for amputees to put stumps where stumps were clearly not intended to go. Every day would be a veritable buffet of bodily fluids and excretions, a catalog of sexual longings and obsessions. These were people who regarded the laws of physics and the limits of bodily contortion as merely strong suggestions.

* * *

But unlike my predecessors, I arrived on the job fully equipped to han-dle even the most salacious parts of personals. There was nothing in the personals that I hadn't already seen with my own two eyes. Bring them on, I told them. I can take it. Finally, all those years of working in a video store were going to serve a higher, more noble purpose.

Everyone who works in a video store likes to think they're a Quentin Tarantino in the making, but I was more of a Larry Flynt.

Other people obsessed over anime from Japan or the works of Ingmar Bergman, but my heart was in the back room, behind the beaded curtain. I knew every detail of every blue movie the store carried; if a customer needed a recommendation—something special, something particular—I was the guy to ask.

Looking for a dirty movie where women chew gum? Got it. Or men sneeze? I had videos with interracial zombies, ice skaters, and elevator repairmen; I could direct the newly divorced to titles featuring women punching and kicking men, or men kicking and punching each other, and I always knew to stock up on videos with sexy little people when the circus was in town. Hard-core porn is the stuff of fantasy, pure and simple—she screams, he screams, you scream, rewind, return. It wasn't a very demanding job. I had a lot of free time. And I watched a lot of porn.

"You know," I'd tell my video-store customers, "real lesbians probably don't have sex in stiletto heels. When the lesbians I know have sex, they mean business—and those heels, they're just plain dangerous. Trust me, if a lesbian is wearing stilettos in bed, somebody's gonna lose an *eye*. And why do the inmates in those hard-core prison videos all have tan lines and lustrous, carefully coiffed hair? Shouldn't they be in lockdown? I'm just saying."

Most people were embarrassed, wanting only to get their dirty movies and get out as fast as possible, but there were people who preferred my recommendations to spending hours wading through boxes covered with enormous fake breasts and buttocks as smooth and shiny as a freshly waxed floor. It was because of my great ability to recommend porn that I got my first writing job—reviewing pornography. It

wasn't such a bad job; it was, in fact, a very good job. My only stipula-
tions were that I wouldn't write under my real name and I wouldn't
write anything dirty. How many ways can a person describe sex? I figured it to be about six. So when I reviewed pornography, I wrote about
everything *except* sex.

"Shyla Diamond," I once wrote, "which I suspect is not her real
name, lives in an enormous, generously appointed mansion located in
what could only be Southern California. Ms. Diamond's latest feature,
Butt Buster Babes 5, is a cautionary tale about the perils of home own-
ership and expensive, albeit poor, decorating choices. A house
requires constant, exhausting upkeep; there are gardeners and repairmen and scantily clad women arriving to read your water meter just as
you're taking a sensuous bubble bath. The parade never ends. In the
penultimate scene, Ms. Diamond entertains both a plumber and an
electrician—union workers, paid by the hour—on what can only be
described as the ugliest sofa in the history of seating. You'll only be
mildly interested in the efforts of Ms. Diamond and her laborers, but
you will not be able to tear your eyes away from that sofa—lime green
with pink stripes and silver dots, I kid you not. Ms. Diamond's decora-
tor clearly lacked the ability even to fake his work, a trait Ms. Diamond,
sadly, seems to share."

It's quite surprising how many dirty movies are made every year,
and it wasn't long before the tapes and disks they sent me to review
began to pile up in my apartment. It wasn't like I could just throw them
in a drawer or hide them in the back of my closet—there were hundreds of dirty movies everywhere you looked, each one clearly and
threateningly marked *"Screener only, not for resale,"* which pretty

much made selling them impossible. Even giving them away became a major chore. A stack of porn doesn't make the best hostess gift, and the Salvation Army doesn't appreciate such a donation, no matter how well-meant. I couldn't even throw the things away—the garbage men asked me to stop.

A guy with three or four thousand hard-core pornographic movies in his apartment is not going to be shocked by anything, except, possibly, sunshine and fresh air. It got to the point where I never wanted to see another naked man or woman again. I'd become completely and utterly jaded, and I never even got off the couch. Thus, faking naïveté wasn't even remotely possible when I began working in the personals. And within days of being hired, I was once again back in the habit of making recommendations and steering product—only now, instead of videos, I was selling people.

*   *   *

But love is more difficult than sex—less sticky, but, oddly, more messy. People who get all squeamish about sex should consider how much worse love really is—there's no process, no money shot; you can have safe sex, but love will always be a dangerous and risky thing. Sex is basic—even incredibly stupid people can figure out how to do it, eventually—but love takes skill, and when you screw up love it hurts. There's no preventive, no magic pill, no vaccine to inoculate you from the dangers of love.

The unnamed woman—Bubbly Earthy—across the counter from me could've used a distemper shot, however. She was on the verge of becoming rabid; her hand was on my hand, and she kept asking me to look at her so she could see my eyes.

"So blue," she said, dreamily. "You have such *blue* eyes. Has anyone ever told you how blue your eyes are?"

I averted my gaze. All I wanted to know, I told her, was her name. She told me, and I immediately wrote it down at the top of her ad.

"No, no," she told me. "It's *Elisabith*, not *Elizabeth*. People do that all the time. E-l-i-s-a-b-i-t-h." I was willing to bet it was "Elizabeth" on her driver's license, but you have to give people their little affectations. It's *Gragg* instead of *Greg*, *D'loris* instead of *Dolores*. Steven is the name of some schlub accountant who takes the bus to work and adds Helper to his Hamburger—but *Stephan* parties with the beautiful people, drives a Lamborghini, and does a little modeling in his spare time, when he isn't dating whomever he damn well pleases. Or so he wants you to think; we get a lot of Stephans in the personals.

"Hello, Elisabith," I said. "I'm Mike."

Knowing tricks like this is why I make the big money.

"So, are you single?" Elisabith asked me, and an embarrassed silence followed. She'd gone from defensive and anonymous to picking out bridesmaid dresses for our wedding, all in a matter of minutes. This sort of thing happens a bit more often than I care to admit, and it's always awkward, to say the least. I'm not much to look at, with the demon eyebrows and the constant smirk; I don't happen to be rich or charismatic or sexy—I just happen to be *present*. It's like thinking the bus driver is actually driving you home.

Beneath the desk, out of view, I was already fumbling to get the ring I keep in my pocket onto my finger—pink and platinum gold, a keepsake from a failed relationship that has proven to be particularly invaluable at awkward moments on the job. Whether I'm seeing someone or not, I keep the ring with me for moments like this.

I held up my left hand for her to see.

"Married," I said.

A long, low noise of disappointment came out of Elisabith— *"Awwwww"*—the howl of too many evenings of microwave dinners for one.

"Married and *gay*," I told her. "It just gets worse and worse, doesn't it?"

She looked a little stunned at that one.

"Oh, *God*," she said.

I smiled apologetically.

"So, you're bisexual?" she asked. "Doesn't your wife . . . ?"

"No," I told her, "I'm married to a man. More or less. As close as— well, you know. Not bisexual. Not into women. Though I like women. As *people*."

"Wait," Elisabith said. "You're kidding, right?"

There was a long pause.

"You've never slept with a woman?"

"Nope."

"Never?" she said, incredulous. "You've *never once* slept with a woman?"

"Nope," I said. "But I've seen it a lot on video."

"Honey," Elisabith told me, "it's not the same thing at all, not by a long shot. You're cute. You don't want to end up a bitter old virgin, do you?"

"I'm hardly a *virgin*," I told her.

"Not according to the Bible," she replied. "It's a rule, I think it's in the old part. 'Thou shalt lie with a woman,' or something like that. Either way, sleeping with guys doesn't count, not to God."

The Bible? A *rule*? The *old part*? I thought about nonchalantly throwing the word *hermaphrodite* into her personal ad—anywhere, where she described either herself or what she was looking for—but I'm not that petty. In fact, I resolved to remove the overabundance of exclamation points ("I love theater and music and good times! I'm looking for a man who's caring and compassionate!"), though I would later misspell the word *intellectual* where she talked about how smart she was, which is always funny.

I figured we were about done here. Bubbly Earthy—I mean *Elisabith*—sighed with resignation, and not a little relief.

"I don't suppose you have any brothers?" she asked.

I smirked.

"Well," I said, "I have a lot of brothers."

"Really?" Elisabith said, much interested.

"But only two are still single. One's a priest—"

"Next."

"I thought as much," I told her. "The other one's a cook. I mean a chef. My brother Colin."

Elisabith mulled it over. "How old is he?"

"We're all two years apart," I told her. "So, he's—let's see, two, four—he's six years younger than I am. Nice guy. Works evenings, but at least you'd know where he is at night."

"Well," she said, collecting her purse and turning toward the door. "Give him my number. And my name." At the door she stopped and turned to me. "But don't tell him you met me through a personal ad— or I'll spill the beans about your lil' 'virgin' problem." And she was gone.

*   *   *

"She sounds like a fuckin' nightmare," Colin said when I called him. "And she's too old for me." He was only half listening, preoccupied with looking for his prized knives—long, sharp, terrifying things that he loves more than life itself. They were somewhere in his kitchen, hidden among the bowls and mixers and cutting boards, but he didn't know where. He usually keeps his knives close, in a brown paper shopping bag, which is why he rarely takes airplanes when he travels. None of us can understand why he's still single.

"Don't work your shit on me, fucker," Colin told me. "There's a real sweet waitress we hired a couple weeks ago that I'm gonna ask out, she's got great cans, so consider me taken."

"Just for clarity's sake," I asked him, "what part are the cans?"

"Boobs," he said.

"Another waitress," I said. "Haven't you worked your way up to hostess yet? Why don't you go ask the coat-check girl out, just to get a little variety?"

"Fuck you, fucker."

"Nice mouth on you," I told him. "You're starting to sound just like Mom."

Colin let out a yelp of joy and pain—he'd found his knives, or else he was finding this conversation annoying. It's hard not to pick on him.

Colin is the youngest of us guys, and that has to be pretty depressing. We're talking about a guy who was always, and would always be, the youngest brother. The teasing and torment was one thing, but imagine knowing, even as a little kid, exactly what you were going to look like and act like when you got older. I know that lately Colin's been watching his older brothers and not liking what's to come—how the hair grows thin and finally departs, how the jowls start, exactly where he'll put on fat. But the pressure to settle down like the others is starting to worry him, I can tell; even the priest brother has a steady thing going with God. And now things had hit a new low: his big gay virgin brother was passing him his rejects.

"All these waitress chicks ever want is sex anyway," Colin said. "Or someone to take care of their kids. Believe me, the sex chicks are easier to deal with."

He said this, but I didn't quite believe him. The sex chicks are easier for *me* to deal with at work, but in life, they aren't quite enough. Colin talks a good game, but he'd rather go hungry than eat garbage, and he knows sex is no substitute for love. He's been trying to find someone for the longest time, but being a chef interferes. Every evening he's in the kitchen with the dishwashers and line cooks, while out front happy couples on dates enjoy his labors. At the end of the night he cleans his ovens and scrubs the pots, and maybe there's a girl, someone easy, no muss, no fuss. But in his heart he longs for something messier.

[9] *Pot Shabbat*

JEWISH SOCIAL GROUP. Looking to meet for services, great conversation around the Kiddush table, and enjoy the company of those who share our faith. It doesn't matter how religious you are. Let's just be friends.

None of us will ever know what really happened between the Fat Chick and the Jewish Guy, but I think I speak for everyone when I say we wish they'd knock it off. One doesn't like overweight women, and the other doesn't like Jews. Fine. We get it. But don't ask us to take sides in your dispute, this little battle you're waging with each other. We got together and we all agree—you're both equally, perfectly awful. There. Are you happy now?

She says she's not fat. He says he's Reform and goes to temple only twice a year. He says she described herself as "curvy" and "proportionate" in her personal ad, and claims that representation was highly inaccurate. She says that he read too much into her words, and that she made a rather unpleasant stereotype about large Semitic noses to make this point. They've each written letters of complaint, which, in keeping with my strict policy of utter ambivalence, I have ignored. Each wants to claim the title of blameless, innocent dupe, and, finding no sympathy in me, both the Fat Chick and the Jewish Guy have taken their grievances directly to my bosses.

They are not pleased. The managing editor, the owners, and the publisher have all been contacted, and they take these matters very seriously indeed. There have been meetings and e-mails sent back and forth, and I've been called into many offices and read the riot act. "How could this have happened?" they ask me. "How did the system fail?" It isn't that they object to anyone being disparaged for being fat or Jewish, that's hardly the issue. What's really troubling is that these people—my people—have been pestering them, which they absolutely cannot abide. Clearly, I'm not doing my job, which is, first and foremost, to keep the personals advertisers as far away from them as possible. Keep the circus in your own tent, they tell me. Make them go away.

"The thing to remember," the publisher instructs me, "is to always smile and nod." It's been decided that this crisis demonstrated that I needed a little refresher in customer service. "Smile and nod, let the people know you're listening. Maintain eye contact. It tells them you're there for them—it tells them you care."

I suggest that such things might not help in the present case, as I have not actually met the Fat Chick or the Jewish Guy in person.

"Just smile and nod. Remember that." And then, finally, I understand. And I smile. And nod.

Business is slow. It's been a long, hot summer in the city, and every-body, including the Fat Chick and the Jewish Guy, obviously has far too much time on their hands. Personally, I've been enjoying the slow-motion soap opera between these two advertisers, and I hope it lasts through August. There's not much else to entertain me. Nobody needs a personal when they can actually interact, live and face-to-face, with other human beings; instead of describing how much they love long walks on the beach, gourmet dining, and lazy Sunday mornings, people are actually putting on their bathing suits, eating out, and sleep-ing in. The offices are very quiet, the heat has driven away advertisers and freelance writers and all the other people of questionable sanity to whom stopping by the offices of a newspaper is a regular habit, and those of us who have no choice but to be here are just sitting in our cubicles, bored and drowsy. A couple of people are playing solitaire at their desks, others are looking at websites or reading other news-papers, and one is sleeping off his usual Friday morning hangover—which is not much different from the hangovers he suffers Monday through Thursday. He's sitting upright in his chair, his hands on the keyboard, and he's facing his computer monitor; from behind it would appear he's hard at work, earning his daily keep. But his head is tilted back ever so slightly, and his eyes are rolled back in his head, half closed in slumber. Occasionally he lets loose a loud snore and jolts awake in his chair, but after nervously looking around to see if the boss is present, he's back asleep, well-rested and probably overpaid.

I know I won't be missed if I leave the office early. There's so much to do; our guests will be arriving just before the sun sets, and I have to get myself to the kosher market on the far north side of the city, which will be jammed, plus I have to pick up flowers and a couple of bottles of rabbi-approved wine. It has been decided that it's okay to send an Irish-Catholic on these missions, because having me do busywork is better than letting me do the cooking. I also need to get a quarter bag: I can't forget that. My dealer says he's gotten some primo stuff in, he won't say from where, but he described it as "a religious experience"— which is exactly what I'm looking for.

Nothing but the best. Because nothing else will do.

I usually smoke substandard stuff, pot that's been cheaped down with oregano and basil; it's the preferred flavor of those of us in low-level publishing careers who can't afford anything better. I didn't really smoke marijuana in high school, nor in college; it wasn't until I worked at a newspaper that I lit up. If it weren't for drugs and alcohol, no one would have anything to read because no one could bear to write.

My introduction to pot came around the same time I discovered religion—not my religion, but the boyfriend's. I never had any real interest in Judaism before the boyfriend, but when you love someone you want to know everything about him; you want to understand all the things that had a hand in shaping him into the person you adore— what his childhood was like, what values he was raised with, all the things that add up to how he sees the world. The boyfriend is smart and talented and driven, he's a good guy—but there are things he says, things he does, that I just don't understand. I don't think these are necessarily "Jewish" things, but there really is a difference between Catholics and Jews, don't let anyone tell you otherwise.

And that difference is Jell-O.

For Jews, Jell-O is an occasional dessert—but for Catholics, it's a regular side dish. I was raised in a house where Jell-O was a staple, always sharing a plate with the entrée, be it spaghetti, pot roast, fish sticks, anything. It was cheap, it was easy to make, and, while it may not have stood up well next to heated foods, its melted, runny Day-Glo colors gave meat loaf and Tater Tots a sorely needed *oomph.* The first time I cooked dinner for the boyfriend, I served chicken wings, white rice, and green Jell-O; this was, not coincidentally, also the last time I cooked dinner for the boyfriend. Jews will eat Jell-O, he told me, but only while hospitalized, and the doctor better have some good credentials. Obviously, Judaism had a lot to teach me, and I was eager to learn.

The boyfriend was not particularly religious when I met him; he wasn't observant, he didn't keep kosher, and he didn't belong to a temple. I certainly wasn't dutifully devout, either—I'd pretty much wrung everything I was going to get out of Catholicism, and didn't much care for the direction the company seemed to be going in. But the longer the boyfriend and I stayed together, the more I began to think about the future.

What's going to happen when we die? I wondered. I wasn't asking this as an existential question; I am a small little man in a big crazy world, and pondering the meaning of life and the workings of the universe seems a little frivolous when there are bills to pay and I can't even figure out where to get a decent haircut. I have no desire to get into a debate over whether or not there is an almighty, all-seeing God; the presumption that He exists seems to me as arrogant and self-serving as the assumption that he—lowercase—doesn't. No, I was fretting about death more as a practical matter—what, specifically, were the boyfriend and I supposed to do?

It was the prospect of unavoidable, horrible death that prompted us to join a temple. We needed something, some kind of support system for all that was to come, and the Catholic Church wasn't going to do the trick. Besides not being too thrilled with the gay thing, Catholics have a tendency to fetishize the dead—we pump our loved ones full of chemicals, paint them up, and put them out on display for a few days, and then throw a big drunken party. The boyfriend didn't like the idea of turning me into a piñata, and neither did I. I'm hoping for something involving a catapult and an angry grief-stricken mob, but I figured that since I'd be dead, my wishes wouldn't really matter.

Joining a shul became much more than just an insurance policy in case of death or dismemberment—we got to know some really interesting people who became very close friends, and these Shabbat dinners are a result. Every month we get together to observe the Sabbath, eat, and smoke dope. The Pot Shabbat dinners came about because our friends didn't want me thinking that kosher law was created thousands of years ago by aliens from outer space, as the boyfriend insisted. They've been an on-again, off-again event for a few years, and while there are sometimes new faces, it's more or less the same three or four couples every time—Robert Shtick and Jimmy Drek (the Shtick-Dreks), David Mach and Murray Schnel (the Mach-Schnels), and Allen Alter and Dan Cocker (the Alter-Cockers). It's our turn to host, the boyfriend and me, and there's no way we can top last month's extravaganza, a luau-themed multicourse soiree that included Hawaiian music and flowery leis for each of the participants. It was beautiful. There will be no theme to tonight's dinner party, no special guest speaker, no gift bags. There will be a few prayers, a brisket, and several communal joints (after the spilling of bong water on a hand-upholstered antique French loveseat, rolled marijuana cigarettes became de rigueur), and, of course, more squabbling and hostility than at all the Christmases I ever had as a child combined.

The Alter-Cockers arrive first, loudly disagreeing about the value of real estate in our part of the city. Allen and Dan are strenuously, unapologetically loud and aggressive, and they revel in it. No matter what they fight about—no matter how small or insignificant the disagreement— they argue as if the fate of the whole world hangs in the balance.

"Allen, you are a fucking idiot," Dan is saying. "A parking space in this neighborhood could not—repeat *not*—ever go for more than twenty-five thousand dollars. You don't know what you're even talking about."

"In a nice condo building, one of the new ones? Easily thirty thousand, more like thirty-five thousand," Dan replies. "Am I right?" It takes me a moment to realize this last question is more or less being directed at me, and I merely shrug.

"I wouldn't know," I tell them as I pour their drinks—vodka martinis, no olives, just the way they like them. "I don't even have a driver's license."

"No! You *can't* not drive." Allen shrieks. "Do you know what happens to people when they get old and don't drive? They end up stuck at home, shut-ins, hermits, ordering in pizza and Geritol, and plenty of Metamucil. The only way they leave is feet first."

"That's a happy thought," I tell them as I hand them their drinks.

"Thanks for that." The boyfriend is peeling and chopping garlic, and he looks up at me, glances at Dan and Allen, and rolls his eyes. We both share a laugh as they go off to the living room to continue their argument.

By the time the Shtick-Dreks and Mach-Schnels arrive, the house is already gauzy with smoke, and the usual hot-button topics are being voraciously debated. These include, but are not limited to, the inadequacies of today's youth and their music, which new restaurants have the worst food and the poorest service, the best gastroenterologists and the impossibility of obtaining an appointment with one, and a topic that never seems to go out of style: celebrities who might be gay.

Once everyone's got a decent buzz on, we move on to friendlier topics, such as religion and the politics of the United States, Israel, and the Middle East. There is a great deal of squabbling, even more interrupting, followed by protestations over having been so rudely interrupted. Our dog, who's been locked upstairs in the bedroom, howls at the din, but she can barely be heard above the shouting. The fights ebb and flow, the volume rising and falling in waves, but it isn't until the table is good and baked that each couple lays into the issue that honestly bothers them the most: each other.

While the Alter-Cockers bicker loudly and passionately over every little thing that annoys each about the other—the snoring at night, the farting, the belching, their mothers—the Shtick-Dreks argue in whispering asides. Perhaps Rob and Jimmy think that by keeping their disagreements muted and hushed, they somehow escape attention, but it is by so obviously trying to appear in harmony that their fights stand out.

"You weren't supposed to say anything about my brother's goiter," Rob hisses at Jimmy. "You promised."

"Relax, none of them have ever even met your brother," Jimmy whispers back. "And could you possibly yap on any more about your super-hot personal trainer? I think we've all heard quite enough about Tito's dreamy eyes and huge calves. You're completely embarrassing me."

"Let's discuss this later, at home."

"Yes, let's do that."

"Hey, guys," Murray calls out sarcastically, his voice thick with drink and weed. "A few people in the back of the second balcony can't hear you. Louder, please."

By the time we get to salads, no couple is sitting together except the Mach-Schnels, mostly because everyone else is afraid to sit next to either of them. David and Murray never raise their voices to each other, never exchange harsh words or cold looks. In fact, they barely interact with each other at all. All there seems to be is a silent tension that builds and builds until all you can think of is how far you have to get away to clear the blast zone. There have been evenings when I've said good-bye to Dave and Murray thinking that that, finally, would be the last time I ever saw either of them alive, let alone together.

Between courses, as we clear plates, I worry to the boyfriend that the police may show up at any moment. I have no idea what the neighbors must think; from the outside we must sound like a riot in progress, or like we're all watching a boxing match or holding a public execution. He hasn't noticed. It's a fairly typical Shabbat dinner, except I'm performing the duties of a boyfriend, and not just the Shabbat goy. As the only gentile present at these affairs, I am often called upon to turn lights on and off, or light the oven. I don't mind. Frenchy Boy the Shabbat Goy. I've been called worse.

There will come a point, usually toward coffee and dessert, when the pot makes everyone sentimental, and the fighting finally dies down. I love this part, when they all reminisce and replay the details of their childhoods, their bar mitzvahs, and stories from summer camp.

"And remember," Rob tells me, "it's not 'summer camp.' It's *Jewish* camp."

"Like you haven't been told a million times already," David adds.

"I went to Hebrew school every day after school," the boyfriend says wistfully. "Mrs. Mankowitz—I'll never forget her. Lithuanian. Thick accent. She wore thick glasses, and her hose were always rolled halfway down her calves. She was always calling my mother to complain about something or another I did. I drove her crazy."

"All I got are nun stories, from Catholic school," I say. "I think I'll save those for Christmas."

We're all just starting to get a little too comfortable when Mindy arrives. Mindy Liebowitz is a woman who does not enter a room demurely. She said that she might be joining us for dessert, and after sitting through Friday evening services with a man she's decided she doesn't like or will see again, she arrives like a hurricane. Mindy is a forty-six-year-old public relations executive, the latest in a long line of jobs she's gotten through her father, with whom she does not speak. She is disheveled and dizzy from the heat, and happy to have missed a heavy dinner of brisket and intercouple sniping.

"How are things with the Bickersons?" she asks us all. "Or should I say the Bickersteins? I tell you, the air in here is full of love."

"That's pot," says Murray. "Want some?"

"I only came here to see *you*," Mindy says, pointing at me. "You need to help me. As only you can."

I assume Mindy needs me to light her cigarette or mow her lawn while she observes the Sabbath, but all she wants is for me to write her a personal ad.

"Since I've dated every Jew within plus or minus fifteen years of my age within a ten-mile radius, I've decided to bite the bullet, stick it out there, and do the ad thing. But I don't want to write it *myself*," she tells me. "Just keep in mind that I don't want to meet any sickos or freaks or prison inmates—been there, done that—so I want you to pick through the responses and send me only the good ones."

"Fine," I tell her. "What do you want? What are you looking for?"

"He's got to have a job," Rob says.

"A good job," the boyfriend adds.

"*Any* job," says Mindy.

"And he's got to be Jewish," Allen adds. "Otherwise, Mindy's father will kill her. Or at least never get her another job." Mindy throws Allen a don't-fuck-with-me look, and inhales deeply from the joint I passed her.

"And he's got to be funny, and sweet, and handsome, right?" Murray asks. "Wish for everything—why not wish for a prince among men? I did."

"Ugh," says David.

"I didn't say I *got* him," says Murray.

"I don't care who he is or what he does," Mindy says, exhaling a cloud of smoke from her nostrils—a gesture that is not particularly attractive. "Just as long as we get along."

All the rest of us look at one another, rolling our eyes and trying not to laugh.

"*Alle yevonim hoben eyn ponim,*" Dan says. "Just look around this table, babycakes."

"What does that mean?" I ask.

"It means 'All Greeks have one face,'" says Dan.

"And what does *that* mean?"

"'Good luck with that'—more or less."

No one has ever explained to me why it takes Jews two hours to say good-bye, but once they've all left, I roll up my sleeves and tackle the dirty plates, pots, pans, and glasses.

"The brisket was too dry," the boyfriend laments.

"Shut up, it was perfect," I tell him. "Everybody said so. You're a great cook."

"You didn't eat any," he says.

"I ate a little. I just prefer my brisket with a big dollop of Jell-O on the side," I say with a smirk. "You know that."

"Lime Jell-O," the boyfriend says.

"No," I correct him. "Not *lime. Green.* Jell-O has colors, not flavors."

"Oh, yeah."

We replay the whole evening, minute by minute—how the food was, how the table looked, all the little things that people talked about and did—and agree that everything seemed to go pretty well. But I mention that I did not like the fighting.

"It bothers me," I tell him. "It makes me feel bad. Do you think any of them are happy? Really happy? They all fight so much. We don't fight like that, do we?"

When the last dish is washed and the glasses are all dried and put away, we climb the steps to the bedroom, exhausted. The dog is waiting for us there, hungry for attention after being cooped up all night, and we lie in bed silently with her, not saying anything.

"Are you happy?" I ask. The question is for both of us, for him and for me, but the boyfriend has already drifted off to sleep, his breathing deep and regular, and the only answer is the dog wagging her tail.

> *JUST FIGURED IT OUT. Bi-leaning-to-gay MWM looking*
> *to meet my first. Tall, average build and good-looking. I like*
> *all the usual stuff. I'm bottom to versatile, I think. I am look-*
> *ing for a long-term relationship only, no one-night stands. If*
> *you're okay with being my first, and last, then I want to hear*
> *from you.*

Now, this was strange. Brad was a familiar presence in the personals; he'd been writing ads for quite a while, and they were always for the same thing: a scantily clad twenty-something woman with loose morals to accompany him to swinger parties. He would specify the female's physical requirements—small hips, large breasts, firm buttocks—as if he were ordering a pizza, while giving only the vaguest description of himself ("nice-looking") and very emphatically insisting that no strings would be attached, no chains would bind, no relationship would ensue. But this new ad was totally out of character, totally out of left field. I never saw it coming.

"I hope you're happy," I told Jeff. "You totally turned some guy gay."

The wheels of Andy's chair squeaked as he quickly rolled himself out of his office and into the hallway, where I was standing outside Jeff's cubicle. Jeff, being both gay and in his twenties, has an office space cluttered with campy postcards, dozens of magazines, and mindless bric-a-brac. When Jeff turned away from his computer to face me, the look on his face was one of amused bafflement.

"What the hell are you complaining about now?" Jeff asked.

"Brad what's-his-face, one of the boring swinger guys—you fucked up his ad two months ago. And now he's gay. Thanks to you."

I'd dug up the ad this Brad guy had written two months previous, and the way Jeff had written it, and I read it out loud as Jeff and Andy listened:

> *SEXY MWM SEEKING adventure. I am looking for a woman who is open to the swinging lifestyle. Be healthy, active and attractive. I want sex only, no strings. We would get to know each other before exploring what's out there. City dweller, prefer same. Serious replies only.*

"That doesn't sound gay," said Jeff. "Not that gay, anyway."

"Yeah, but you dropped the 'looking for' at the beginning of the second sentence," I said. "'*I am a woman who is open to the swinging lifestyle*'—and who do you think responded to him? A bunch of guys who thought he was a woman. I'm guessing he hit it off with one of them—at least—and one thing led to another and—"

"Well shit, that's not my fault," Jeff said.

"Yeah," said Andy. "The dude must've been at least a little gay before, right? Why would he agree to go meet some guy who thought he was a woman?"

"Maybe he didn't," I told them. "But apparently the guys who answered his ad got him to thinking about it, because now he's placing an ad looking for a guy."

I showed them the ad I'd gotten in the mail.

" 'Bi-leaning-to-gay'?" Andy snorted. *"Right."*

"And this is still my fault?" Jeff asked sourly.

"Big homo," said Andy.

"Yeah, thanks to Jeff," I responded. "So he's going to meet some guy, and they'll agree it's going to be strictly sex—nothing more, nothing less. And then it'll be a couple of beers and then sex. And then dinner and a little sex. And then they'll go to a hockey game together. And then they'll go camping. And then it will be too late. Too. Damn. Late."

"Has he called you?" asked Jeff. "Has he asked you to switch him back? Wave your big fairy wand and make it all go away?"

"Maybe you should give him a refund," Andy suggested. We were all three of us very quiet for a moment, and then Andy started laughing and Jeff joined in and I couldn't hold my fake-boss composure any longer. We all shook our heads at the insanity of it.

I never give refunds and they both know it.

*   *   *

I am no expert on the human heart, nor do I pretend to be. The boys and I witness a lot of strange behavior every day, and we're all at a loss to explain or make sense of most of it. Knowing what I do for a living, people will oftentimes offer me the chance to pontificate on the mysteries of love and desire, but I am hardly equipped to do so. It would seem to be a matter best left to poets, playwrights, and heavy drinkers—they try, but even they must inevitably throw up their hands in sputtering, wordless frustration. Scientists have given it their best shot, trotting out graphs and charts, testing and rejecting theories, attempting to demonstrate that love is a quantifiable matter of socioeconomics and codependence, while longing is nothing more than a measurable production of pheromones and sweat glands—but such explanations, in their coldness and rationality, rarely satisfy.

It's not even that love and lust defy explanation and expectation; it's that they are so often diametrically opposed. There are those to whom love is, and always must be, attachment unencumbered by the mechanics of sex—pure, chaste, absent of sweating or moaning. And then there's the group that crashes into heartbreak again and again, always assuming carnal lust to be something more than a simple craving, not unlike what some people feel for chocolate or sports cars.

The guy who promised he'd call and never did; the woman who needs medication and a restraining order to be kept at bay; the husband whose eyes fixate on every pretty girl who happens by; and the wife with the constant migraine headache. So many unhappy, unsatisfied people—what's going on here? Is it global warming? Violence in video games? Fluoride in the water? The liberal media? The Republican National Committee? Certainly, the Republicans are never part of the solution, but I would suggest an explanation that's far more reasonable, logical, and rational than any of the above: fairies.

· That's what my mother would call them, anyway. She believes in all that old Irish horseshit—fairies and unicorns and banshees. What I call fairies, the ancient Greeks called gods. I studied Greek when I was in college, and I was consistently a solid C student, so I know of what I speak. If I'm correct, and I'm fairly sure I am, the entire problem of love and lust was definitively explained thousands of years ago through Greek mythology—it's all there, if you'd bother to look. Sure, it's a little confusing, like watching a Spanish soap opera with no knowledge of Spanish or Latin culture, and yet finding it entertaining—there's a lot of sex, a lot of religion, and then there's more sex. Especially in my favorite story, the tale of Eros and Himeros.

The waters swirled and churned and turned upon themselves, this way and that, and from the foam of the sea came forth Aphrodite—the goddess of beauty and rapture, whose name would be appropriated by many prostitutes and porn starlets for millennia to come. There's a famous painting of Aphrodite standing naked in an open clamshell with her hands demurely covering her private parts; above her are two adorable little cherubs, one on each side, sent to guard and protect her. These are Eros and Himeros.

Eros is the god of love, true love, the long-term, grow-old, bury-us-next-to-each-other thing.

Himeros is the god of desire. The cheap fling.

The Romans stole Eros and Himeros and turned them into fat babies with wings, and eventually folded them into one all-purpose god named Cupid, who went on to fame and fortune in the figurine and Valentine's Day card racket. But for the Greeks, who started it all, Eros and Himeros were not charmingly pudgy little tots but surly teenagers looking for trouble. Teenagers with wings, armed with bows and arrows. Terrifying. Moreover—and this is the whole point—Eros and Himeros looked exactly alike; no one could tell them apart. The Trojan War began because Paris thought it was Eros who led him to Helen—but, surprise, it was Himeros, playing tricks. The meaning of the tale is clear: you might say you're in love, you might even think you're in love, but, in fact, you might just be horny. You have to love a religion that not only acknowledges the difference but deifies it.

None of this helps, of course. But it absolves Jeff, Andy, and me of all responsibility in the Brad affair, and all affairs of love and lust, for that matter, and that's something, at least. The sizzling romance that grows cold and stale after three dates, the crazed stalker waiting outside your office, the returned engagement ring and unreturned phone call—it's not your fault, you're off the hook. It's nice when hot and heavy turns out to be solid and steady, but such things are exceptionally rare. Some people are lucky; the rest of us are fools of the gods.

Which at least gives Jeff, Andy, and me something to talk about. Andy will occasionally make it clear that the only thing keeping him from dumping his girlfriend is that they can't keep their hands off each other, while Jeff will imply that the intimacy between him and his boyfriend includes everything except sex. I say nothing, but we all know my home life includes neither affection nor lust. Most of the time we avoid talking about ourselves altogether—an easy thing to do, with advertisers like Brad abruptly switching teams.

"Maybe he just got bored," Jeff suggested. "Though I'm not sure how that's even possible."

"Nah," I told him. "He's confused. He thinks just because his lust for women came up empty, he ought to try showing love for his fellow man instead; it's perfectly understandable." And I let out a long, sympathetic sigh.

"He just confused his fairies," I added, and I could see the smirk spread across Andy's face.

"And now," Andy said, "he is one."

JUST SAY NO to babes, bimbos and screeching barflies. Seeking female whose idea of hanging out means staying at home or going for a walk, either in the city or 'burbs. Let's be serious but fun, learn from each other, grow old with each other. SWM 33 is ready and willing to be the man of your dreams. Are you willing to be my girl?

The most common explanation people have for placing a personal ad is that they are sick and tired of what is commonly referred to as the "bar scene." What they really mean is that they have gotten too old, or that they're fed up with smelling like stale beer and full ashtrays, or that they've recently joined a 12-step program. *C'est la vie*. More business for me. But I believe, heart and soul, that bars are given short shrift when it comes to matters of the heart. One always hears about the bar pickups that go wrong—the groggy, hungover awareness at the first light of dawn that you're missing a kidney, that you've been sold into white slavery, that you're lying next to your sister—but the successful matches prompted by one too many gin and tonics or ten too many beers are far more common.

There are, of course, rules about how to find love in a bar successfully. The first, and absolutely most important, is to *tip your bartender*. No one who's stiffed a bartender has ever found happiness, nor should they. Bartenders work very hard under difficult circumstances; they stand for hours at a time, making idle chitchat about sports, politics, or the weather, and anyone who resents the idea of rewarding them for their efforts will inevitably find themselves going home with nothing more than a microwavable burrito. What's more, research has proven that the quality of people you meet is directly relative to the size of your gratuity. If your heart is set on marrying some desiccated corpse with a hacking cough, horrible body odor, a distinctly flabby neck wattle, and rummy, bloodshot eyes, fine, be my guest—but know this: had you left only a couple of bucks more on the bar, things might have turned out very different.

It's also extremely important that you never go to a bar alone. There are a number of reasons for this; one would hate to wake up with a hangover and no kidneys, obviously, but more important is to have someone around with whom to compete. Bars, nightclubs, and pubs often provide a variety of games for their patrons—darts, pool, pinball—but no contest is more satisfying than managing to go home with the object of your friend's affections. There's just something cruelly fulfilling about snagging the chick whom your buddy's been buying drinks for all night, or leaving your girlfriend livid and in tears when the guy she's been swooning over offers to drive you home; it's not your fault he didn't make his move—and she's a big girl, she can find her own ride somehow, right? They'll never forgive you, at least not until next Saturday night, when they steal away whomever it is *you've* been pining for.

Personal ads are great, but don't give up on the bar scene. Good and decent people meet and fall in love in bars all the time. My parents met in a bar. My brother Pat met his lovely wife, Blessie, in a bar. One of my sisters-in-law, probably the nicest of them all, is rumored to have first met my brother outside a bar; I heard he was puking in the parking lot, which was not an unusual activity for any of my brothers during college, and the wave of nausea and pity she felt for the guy turned out to be, in fact, love. I imagine she saw him there, hunched over, losing his cookies, and in her heart she knew—she loved him, she needed him, and she could fix him.

*   *   *

Some people drown their sorrows, while others seem awash in joy. But for my brother Colin, life is constantly dry and sober, no matter if times are good or bad. Diagnosed as a diabetic at the tender age of four, Colin cannot imbibe like the rest of us; his relationship with alcohol is as complicated as his relationship with women—and a person cannot help but think that the absence of one is inextricably related to the absence of the other.

It's a shame. He is, in so many ways, a perfect man. The last of a long line of brothers, Colin was the final chance my parents had to get it right. Whereas Jack, being the oldest, is a man who's responsible, conventional, and confident, Colin, being the youngest, thinks outside the lines, entertains doubt, and changes direction accordingly. While Patrick values financial security and works hard for material comforts, Colin lives happily as a pauper, free of possessions and their limitations, defining his success in much more esoteric, abstract ways. My brother Matt and I, being middle children in such a large group, are content to hide in the background, lost in the crowd, uncomfortable with attention or recognition—but Colin refuses to go unnoticed; when the world is silent, Colin shouts, and when everyone else screams, Colin stands silent, front and center, until he has the undivided attention of everyone in the room. And unlike Casey, whose seriousness, thoughtfulness, and goodness befit his position as a Jesuit priest, Colin is silly, manic, and unabashedly juvenile, riding the wave of high blood sugar or a fresh injection of insulin, reveling in dirty jokes and funny voices, never worried about looking stupid or offending delicate sensibilities.

"Joke 'em if they can't take a fuck," he told me once. That, in a nutshell, pretty much sums the guy up.

All the nieces and nephews love Uncle Colin insanely, and they mob him like a rock star whenever they see him, pulling him to the floor and piling all over him, shrieking with laughter. He's far and away the most beloved and adored of the uncles, which sparks both admiration and jealousy in me. No one wants to show me their favorite toy, or read them a story, or teach them swear words—but, then again, I could never do such things as well as Colin does them.

Colin and I are close, though neither of us has the time or the money to talk as much as we'd like to. Colin loves being a chef, and our conversations usually center on what's happening at his restaurant— how many line cooks he's fired that week, which waitress or sous chef he's been lusting after and rejected by, what rare spice or seasonal ingredient he's currently enraptured by. Colin knows I cannot cook and rarely eat out, so I suspect he's indulging me, sharing a subject he clearly loves just to make me feel included. When he talks about the wonders of tarragon and the proper season for shellfish, I'm out of my element, and I can only make encouraging noises to hide my absolute ignorance; his knowledge of food and discerning palate make it hard to believe we grew up in the same household.

"You have to try vanilla with black pepper," Colin says. "With reduced lemon juice. Try it on baby octopus. Really, it's fuckin' fantastic, your tongue will never know what hit it."

"Mmm," I say. "Sounds great. Do you remember how Mom used to put slices of American cheese on open-face hotdog buns, and then put them under the broiler until the cheese was completely burned and black? That was always fancy, I thought."

Our mom was not the best cook. In fairness, her mother wasn't much of a pro in the kitchen, either—and they were the descendants of a long line of Irishwomen whose culinary skills were confined mostly to boiled meats, overcooked potatoes, and salt. That a woman with only the most meager of culinary skills, raised as an only child in a one-parent household, was forced to feed eight children, her mother, her husband, and various hangers-on each and every day for years is truly the stuff of tragedy; fallen souls in hell are given lighter punishments. But we had to eat her cooking—scorched pot roasts, raw spaghetti, piles of fish sticks that were either soggy and cold or blackened to a crisp. Had it not been for Jell-O, none of us would have survived to adulthood; the only thing Mom really knew how to make were gin and tonics—and that was only because she had some inkling of what the ingredients were.

A lot changed after Colin was diagnosed as a diabetic. Sugar and sweets were immediately taken out of all our diets—we would all eat as he did; Mom was determined that Colin wouldn't be made to feel strange or different from the rest of us in any way. Food, which had been a burden for Mom and a source of unending complaint for the rest of us, overnight became a matter of family loyalty and honor. We choked down every morsel and pronounced it delicious—and when it was horrible, truly and utterly unspeakably horrible, we couched our language in euphemisms.

"This meat loaf is really *interesting*," my sister Anne would say. "Don't you think this tastes *interesting*? This is probably the most *interesting* meat loaf I've ever had."

"I've never tasted anything like it," Casey would say, just a little too brightly.

"Why, look—Matt's already finished," Pat would say. "Dear brother, please take what's left of mine. You're a growing boy, after all, and I *insist*."

"Oh, I couldn't *possibly*," Matt would say. "Really, I just *couldn't*."

And Mom would sit at the head of the table, glaring at the lot of us, the ice in her gin and tonic clinking furiously as she spun the glass around and around, faster and faster.

"Maybe we'll have it again tomorrow, then," she'd hiss. "Since you all seem to like it so much."

Meals were always preceded by Colin's insulin injection—a major event. We'd all gather round, Mom would fill the syringe, and Colin would close his eyes and cover his mouth as she poked the needle into his arm or leg or butt while we all cringed in horror. Colin would eventually learn to do this all by himself, privately and out of sight, but in those early years the task fell to Mom, and I was never sure whom to feel sorrier for—Colin or Mom. I think she would have willingly tied herself to the stove twenty-four hours a day if it had meant never having to stick another needle in Colin.

I've always suspected that it was this strange relationship with Mom that eventually prompted Colin to become a chef. Cooking was something she obviously didn't enjoy but had to do, and maybe Colin— either consciously or unconsciously—learned to cook as a way of thanking her, of paying her back. When he would visit my parents, he'd arrive with a goat in the back of his truck, which he would roast to perfection, or bags of beautiful organic tomatoes that he'd serve to them with mozzarella newly flown in from Italy, or gorgeous fillets of salmon caught wild in Alaska, or dry-aged steaks from Argentina, everything fresh, everything the best. Dad would shake his head and criticize Colin for spending his money on such frivolous, indulgent things— but Mom would sit in the corner of her kitchen, watching, proudly amazed, not quite believing a son of hers could so confidently know his way around a kitchen.

My taste buds are far more welcoming of protein shakes and microwave popcorn, meals that are thoughtlessly easy to make and hardly require the annoyance of "savoring" or appreciating their "subtle delicacy"—so when Colin pontificates about food, I know to keep my mouth shut. Eventually he will tire himself out, and we'll move on to a topic about which I have a bit more authority.

"So, how's your love life?" I ask. "Are you seeing anyone?"

What follows, initially, is a stream of consciousness that will include such words as *chicks, cans, boobs, hotties,* and *goddamn bitches.* Any normal woman listening would be justifiably horrified and rightfully outraged, but this is not the real Colin. This is just the way he talks, a sort of preamble that must be performed before any meaningful conversation takes place. It's like primal-scream therapy; I know when he's through by the long pause and a sigh, immediately followed by the word *anyway.*

"Anyway," Colin says at last, "I've been trying Internet dating again. Match-up-dot-com, Hook-up-dot-com, Marry-me-I'm-fuckin'-desperate-dot-com—all the big ones."

I make a gagging noise, like I'm vomiting. He knows how I feel about those things.

"Don't be angry," he says. "I know they're your archenemies."

"I'm sure there are some very nice, normal people who find dates through the Internet," I tell him. "I'm sure there are some lovely people out there who, even though they cannot spell or use proper punctuation, deserve someone to make them happy. Just because a person types in all-capital letters doesn't mean they're screaming insane freaks who need to be heavily medicated or institutionalized. The Internet's great; you can sit in front of your computer all day and all night, and it's almost—*almost*—like you have a real life. I'm sure you're meeting some really great ladies."

"Well," Colin says, "not really."

"What a surprise."

Colin has been on more lousy dates than just about any man I know, and, remember, I'm at ground zero when it comes to stories about dates gone wrong. Perhaps it's because he works evenings at his restaurant—women who share his schedule, or can at least accommodate his odd hours, are extremely rare. A lot of people work nights, but Colin must be meeting all the bad ones. Sometimes these women are the wrong fit for him, and sometimes he's just completely and totally wrong for them—a dilemma that exists between all men and women who try, and fail, to couple.

"You just need to turn that bug light off," I tell him.

"What?" he says. "What the fuck are you talking about?"

"Your bug light—you're attracting nothing but bugs, losers, the worst that's out there. It's hanging there over your head, and they just swoop in—and then, *zap*. You gotta turn that thing off, man."

It's a twisted fact of life: the very best people always seem to be a magnet for the very worst. Beautiful, kind, vivacious women are inevitably chased by trollish, greasy, stupid guys with dirty fingernails and no jobs, while the handsome, decent, good-hearted men are magnets for nasty shrews who withhold sex and rip apart self-esteem.

Colin has had blind dates with plenty of these women, and they occasionally even bring along their children—hey, someone has to feed those kids. There was one memorable blind date he had with a woman who actually brought her parents. There have been women who abandoned him in restaurants because he dared to order meat, women who lied about their age and blamed it on menopause, women who tearfully confessed that they were still hung up on their ex-boyfriends, or assured him they were on the verge of asking their husbands for divorces. He's been rejected by women because of the car he drives, the clothes he wears, and his wild, unkempt hair. Colin has been told he's too fat, too thin, speaks too quickly, and ought to get a real job. Of course, he's done his fair share of rejecting too—aside from the obviously insane and hopelessly unattractive, there are two big subjects about which he's proven to be utterly inflexible: religion and food.

Colin doesn't discriminate against any woman based on religion, but he absolutely cannot abide churchy, pious types, regardless of their faith. He has no problem calling out ignorance passing for transcendence, or shameful bigotry cloaking itself as victimization; being religiously observant is one thing, but incessant yapping about it is quite another. Let Jesus Christ get his own dates. It is quite likely that Colin knowingly opens his filthy mouth and lets loose a string of profanity simply to weed out such types.

"She told me that she'd pray for me," he said about one such girl. "I asked her if that meant a fuck was out of the question, but I pretty much knew the answer already."

Food is a more complicated matter. It's not about how much a woman eats, or how little she eats, or really even what she eats. This is hardly an empty sentiment, coming as it does from a man who must constantly monitor his blood-sugar level. But women who wallow at the trough, mindlessly stuffing themselves silly, drive Colin crazy; women who refuse to eat anything, and cannot stop talking about whatever it is they're not eating, make him furious. He doesn't know exactly how to put it—a woman who's neither too fat nor too thin, who's neither too full nor too empty—but he knows it when he feeds her. Cooking dinner for someone he's interested in is a very big deal for Colin—and, sadly, few women have made it past dessert.

The guy keeps trying, though—he meets women through the Internet, through friends, even through customers at his restaurant. I've asked him if he wants me to look for women through the personals, and he's voiced a tentative willingness.

There are incredibly nice, normal, wonderful women who place personal ads every day with me—women whom I could easily and enthusiastically recommend to any man who wanted to meet women. But when I read these ads with my brother Colin in mind, I suddenly adopt standards so outlandishly high that no woman could possibly meet them. Moreover, I start reading the ads hypercritically; every word contains a hidden meaning to be dissected and examined.

"She sounds good," I'll say to myself, having picked out an ad from a woman of Colin's approximate age and temperament. "But what does she mean by 'bubbly'? Bubbly is *this* close to 'jolly'—and jolly equals weight problem. Or maybe she drinks too much. Bubbly—obviously, she's trying to say she's a raging, totally out-of-control alcoholic. Well, that won't do for Colin, that just won't do; I can't throw some drunken, wild fat girl at him, that's for sure. Especially because Colin doesn't drink."

We all crave things—a cold beer, a hot date, chocolate, sugar—and abstinence just makes the need ache harder. There is nothing worse than wanting what you cannot have, and all Colin wants is a little sweetness in his life. He can take it, and deserves it, and some nice girl deserves him. He's a good catch—and he's had all his shots.

I've been lately thinking of suggesting he try bars. He's been aiming to find the right girl, experimenting with different flavors and combinations, attempting to get the ingredients for romance just right—but what I think Colin needs is to really concentrate on pairings, douse himself with insulin and open up a few bottles, until he finally feels that warm glow, that sensation of giddiness that makes everything spin. Just as long as he remembers to tip, he'll find a girl worthy of being brought home to meet the family—otherwise, he might end up with someone horrible, someone wretched. Someone bubbly.

"You fucking idiot," I'd whisper in his ear, pulling him aside. "I said a *Bud Light.*"

[1 2] *The Game of Life*

SEEKING TAINTED LOVE. BM 38, attractive, somewhat intelligent, nice guy, seeking long-term relationship with kinky yet sweet, affectionate down and/or out lady. Not pretty? Plump? Dumb? Let me be your knight in shining armor. Let me teach you and always make you feel good. Please respond.

When we're not typing or fielding phone calls, most of what we do at work—Jeff, Andy, and I—is sit around and wonder about the lives of the people who place personals ads. Despite all the customers we know, love, and/or hate, the vast majority of advertisers are strangers, peoples whose lives we can only speculate about while we slack around the office. It's weird how people can tell you their most private desires and deepest wishes, how they can tell you very specific facts about who they are and what they want, and yet they still remain anonymous— even when you know their names and addresses.

"Do you remember the name Joe Palmson?" Jeff asked me. "Do you remember who that was?"

"Of course," I said. "That's one of John Larson's pseudonyms. It's the name he used for his 'I want a wife and children' personal. That's easy. But do you remember the other three names he's used?"

"George Levin," Jeff replied.

"Correct! And?"

"Jesse Palmer and . . . shit, I always forget that other one. . . . " Jeff furrowed his brow, trying to remember.

"*Tick, tick, tick,*" warned Andy.

"It's the name he used in the ad where he said he was 'filthy rich and willing to spoil'—the one where he was looking to get spanked," I hinted.

"That ain't fair," Andy protested. "You can't give the sucker hints." We are, apparently, all suckers. Jeff, Andy, me, the people who place the ads and the people who answer them—dupes, chumps, saps. Names don't matter, age is irrelevant, and not even gender makes a difference. We're nothing but suckers.

"Uh—Murray? It was Murray something. Murray Peterson!"

"Bingo!" I exclaimed. "Way to go, sucker."

I'm not sure if what we're doing is gossiping, making fun, or what—but it feels competitive, like a sport. We don't keep score in this game, and there aren't any rules or winners or losers; it's merely a contest of knowledge and discovery. I doubt the advertisers realize that we pay such close attention to them, and I'm pretty sure they wouldn't like it if they did. We follow the regulars week by week, taking note of what they say and how they say it, and debating what might be going on in their lives. We're not a sequestered jury; we talk about our customers constantly—sometimes with derision, sometimes with admiration, but always with a fascination that reveals just how little we actually have to do during the workday. And, we each have our greatest hits—stories about customers that we never tire of telling one another.

Jeff always likes to tell the tale of Bodybuilder Pierre—mostly because it never fails to embarrass me. Pierre's English was not so good, but he knew just enough to make it clear that he had the hots for me.

"Oh, he had it *bad*," Jeff said. "He couldn't go two days without coming to see you, remember? And he was just the ugliest fucker in the world."

"What was wrong with his skin?" asked Andy. "He had just the worst skin, and those big googly eyes—he looked like Harpo Marx." There was something clearly wrong with Pierre; maybe it was from the years of obvious and excessive steroid abuse, but somewhere along the way his brain had turned to mush.

"He sent you that video, remember?" Jeff said. "That one where he has to have his legs tied up over his head because they were too big, and then he stuffed that—"

"*Okay*, yes, we all know what he did," I interrupted. "We watched, we screamed, we destroyed the tape—and I thought we agreed never to mention it again. Didn't we agree to that?"

"Yeah," said Andy. "But then he sent you those pictures of himself in the Catholic schoolgirl's uniform—"

"Oh, *God.*" Will I ever forget the sight of big ol' Pierre, a 210-pound bodybuilder, in a wig, lipstick, and high heels, posing provocatively and winking at the camera? Just the memory of those pictures makes me cover my eyes with my hands.

"Remember Jeff and Margaret?" Andy said. "I'm still amazed she didn't kill him with her bare hands." Margaret was a problem customer who'd been around since the late 1970s; we knew this from her hairstyle, which was long and feathered, inspired by Farrah Fawcett circa 1978. Margaret's hair instantly took you back to the days of disco, which may have also been when she'd actually been a nice, normal, healthy young lady. Late-era Margaret was anything but; she had grown angry and bitter, and developed a very obvious drinking problem. For some reason, Jeff took it upon himself to help her out.

"Well, God—she was such a fucking bitch," Jeff said. "Somebody had to do *something*."

That "something" was to tell Margaret that she was a big, sloppy drunk and that she needed to get some help. Men, Jeff informed her, don't like drunks. He told Margaret that she was rude, that she slurred her words when she talked, and that she smelled like cheap bourbon. No man wants a woman like that, Jeff said, and she needed to either make a change or else stop coming in and wasting his time.

"I'm all about tough love," Jeff said.

Had our bosses known what Jeff had said to Margaret, they'd have fired him instantly. The truth is a big no-no in our line of work, and newspapers are supposed to keep their distance from the people who read and use them. Luckily, the owners, stockholders, and various layers of management have lately been more concerned with rapidly dwindling circulation and loss of ad pages. There have been a lot of meetings held and committees formed, and the only thing the three of us agree on is how glad we are to be uninvolved.

"We'll be fired first," I pointed out. But none of us seems to care that much.

I don't think I know anyone who works here more intimately than I know Andy and Jeff—nor does anyone at the paper know me better. And that's a shame, because a lot of the problems newspapers are having nowadays come from the fact that people aren't possessive or connected to their work. People who own and manage newspapers want to get rich; people who write for newspapers want to be famous. But people like us, who work for newspapers, even in the tiniest role, love newspapers—we read as many as we can, and pass them around, and worship the great ones. Sadly nobody's reading newspapers anymore.

"Maybe it's because of the Internet," Andy said. "Everybody's foaming at the mouth about blogs and the Internet and whatnot stealing away advertisers and readers."

"That is bullshit," I said. "Newspapers just want to please, and sell. They're just content to be absolutely, totally irrelevant. Remember September eleventh?"

Both Jeff and Andy groaned. They've heard me go off on this particular subject dozens of times.

"Not a word," I sneered. "Not one fucking word. Our paper comes out two days after, and it's like nothing happened at all. There's no mention of it anywhere, except in the personals. And do you know why? Because most of the editorial department scrammed. They *left*. *They work at a newspaper!* Insane. *We* were here. *We* stayed the whole day, taking ads and answering the phones. And we're *nobodies.*"

"I hated that day," Andy said. "All those guys trying to use a national tragedy to pick up women. How many personal ads did we take that said stuff like 'During these dark times, nobody should be alone'— how creepy is that?"

"Calm down," Jeff told me. Years have gone by, but I'm still angry about the whole thing.

"Speaking of years ago," Andy sid, "do you remember that guy we used to call Gummy?"

"Oh, God," Jeff said. "The denture guy. I mean, the guy who'd take his dentures out. Whatever happened to him?"

"Yech," I said. "I don't know, and I don't care. He was really old, though. He might have died."

"Didn't you set him up with the 'Eight Throbbing Inches Needs TLC' guy once?" Andy asked. "I loved that guy. What a stupid ad. Eight throbbing inches!"

"Maury, that's who that was," I replied. "No, Maury was straight."

"Oh, that's too bad," Andy sighed. "They would've been perfect for each other. Gummy and Throbby."

"Have you heard from Estelle yet today?" Jeff asked.

"Which one?"

"Not Dinner Whore Estelle," Jeff said. "Does she even call? No, I mean your girlfriend, Estelle What's-her-name."

"Epstein," I replied. "She called yesterday. She went on a date with some fellow who kissed her on a Ferris wheel."

"Aw," said Jeff.

"Yuck," said Andy.

"She goes on more dates than anybody I know," I said. "Or maybe it's just that she's always calling me to tell me about them. For someone who's cheating on her husband, she doesn't seem too careful."

"Isn't she like seventy years old or something?" Jeff asked. "She's not having sex with all these guys, is she?"

"*Tramp*," Andy snickered.

"She's in her sixties, I think," I said. "And she never talks about sex—and since she talks about everything, I kind of assume she's not bedding these guys. Or maybe she is. I don't want to think about it."

"What, you got something against bony old ladies having sex?" Jeff laughed. "Just imagine, their sagging skin and liver spots—I bet they do it with the lights on and the shades open."

"You can get a lot of action out of those artificial hips, you know," Andy said.

"Anyway," I said. "Change the subject."

"Okay," Jeff said, "I got a lovely pair. Though I'm afraid to even say their names."

"Uh-oh," Andy said. "I know who you're thinking of. Don't say it!"

"Who?" I asked.

"They're evil," Jeff said. "Their name is cursed. You told us never to mention them in your presence again, after that last time."

"Oh," I said, and made a face. "The Sumos."

"Don't say the name!" Andy screamed.

"Don't worry. You have to say it three times before they appear," I replied. "Like that movie. You know the one—what was it, *Candyman* or something?"

"God, I hated them" Jeff said.

"Me too," said Andy.

There was something deeply wrong with the Sumos—so named because they looked and acted like a pair of Japanese wrestlers. Both were maybe five feet tall, and at least five feet wide, two nearly perfect spheres doomed to circle around each other, and compete with each other, forever. The Sumos both wore their long, stringy hair tightly pulled back, as befits Japanese wrestlers, and they had enormous mouths accentuated with copious amounts of bright red lipstick, which always found its way to their cheeks and teeth. But what everyone noticed about the Sumos, the thing that struck you first, were the outfits. The Sumos made their own clothes, eye-popping matching ensembles cobbled together from odd bits of fabric, leftover brocade, appliqué flowers, beads and fringe, all of it held together with duct tape and staples.

The Sumos were not twins; then weren't sisters or cousins or relations at all. None of us knew what the deal was with the Sumos, where they came from or how they found me, but as they appeared nearly identical, and shared the same crazy temperament, we always thought of them as a unit. They never placed personal ads, but they always came to the singles parties.

Singles parties. Every so often someone up in management would decide that we needed some way to promote the personals—and what would be more fun than to gather all the sociopaths, outcasts, and rabble of the personals together in one place and have an open bar? It was never less than a recipe for disaster, always bringing out the very worst behaviors in the very worst people. But no one was worse than the Sumos.

"Remember that party where they stole all the food?" Andy said. "Their fat little fingers grabbing everything. They emptied the whole buffet table into garbage bags, slung them over their shoulders, and walked out without saying a word." There were other incidents, including the gentleman who got a face full of red wine when he refused to vacate a table that the Sumos wanted, and the lady who was pushed to the floor because she was blocking the route the Sumos were taking, together as always, to the ladies' room. They were a terror, always cornering us at these events, pulling on our sleeves and jabbing their fingers in our chests, telling us everything that was wrong with men, lecturing about how awful it was to be single, sharing with us how hard it was to be an attractive woman in the big city. Jeff and Andy and I actually started to look forward to the Sumos' presence, just for the pleasure of regaling each other with the lunacy of the encounter later.

Sadly, I had to ban the Sumos from the singles parties after they called the party planner a bitch. It was a shame, because the party planner really *was* a bitch, but complaints were made to management, and management had meetings, and meetings led to committees and, in the end, it was decided that the Sumos weren't so much pleasurably insane as they were just plain no longer welcome. I pleaded their case—it was hardly fair to accuse the Sumos of ruining everyone's good time, because nobody ever had a good time at these parties anyway, and at the very least, the Sumos made other people look better by comparison. But I was overruled.

"Wasn't one a teacher or something?" Jeff asked.

"No way," said Andy.

"High school special education," I told them. "The other was a telephone operator."

"Whatever happened to them?" Andy wondered. "They just sort of fell off the face of the earth."

"I don't know what happened to the one." I told them. "But the telephone operator got married last year."

Jeff and Andy just stood there with their mouths hanging open.

" I *think* it was the operator anyway," I added. "It's not like I could tell those two apart."

"You're fucking with us now," Jeff finally said. Andy's eyes were bulging in mock horror.

"Who?" Jeff demanded. *"Who married a Sumo?"*

"Please don't say the name," I reminded him.

"Nobody could stand them," Jeff said. *"We* couldn't stand them. Nobody would marry a Su—I mean, nobody would marry *one of them,* not even by accident."

"Well, somebody did."

"Are you saying," Andy finally asked, "that the set has been broken up?"

"Yup," I said. "Last year, in June."

Andy made a gagging noise.

"I told her to try JDate, that website for Jewish singles, and she found somebody right off the bat. The other Sumo was a bridesmaid. She sent us a wedding invitation; it's up on the wall of my office. I have no idea who the guy is or what he's about, but I hope they're happy and that we never have to see them again."

"That means there's still one left," Jeff said.

"Still one in the game," Andy said. "Who have we got that we could match her up with?" And the three of us stood there, lighting new cigarettes, playing matchmakers instead of going inside and doing our jobs.

RELEASE COMING SOON. Inmate in Meritville Correctional Center seeking sexy, stunning and sympathetic female with whom to celebrate my re-entry to the free world. Specifically, I mean sex. Inmate has paid his debt to society for Non-Violent offense, I'm also handsome and in good shape. Please send photo and correspondence c/o this newspaper, and they will forward onto me. Let's both get off for good behavior.

Dear Mike Beaumier/ Personals Editor:

Hello! This is Arthur Ratner, inmate #B65833 of Meritville Correctional Center. So we meet again! We do have a tendency to meet under the strangest of circumstances, don't we? (ha ha!) I'm in high hopes that you're doing better than I am in this dungeon. The whole prison is currently in lockdown, because some foolish inmate physically assaulted some prison guard, and we'll probably be on this lockdown for at least 30 more days (what fun!)

All inmates are confined to their cells during a lockdown. This includes for showers, meals, phone calls, visits, etc. etc.—it's very hard. I've been spending my time writing a new personal advertisement, which I have enclosed. The title of my ad, "Hot Sex Pistol," should definitely catch a few onlookers and maybe get me some letters. The fact that I start my parole next August should help me out more this time around. Please make any punctuation or spelling corrections if it is necessary. And thank you for everything!

Respectfully,

Arthur Ratner,

inmate #B65833

Dear Mr. Ratner:

Enclosed please find three letters received in response to your new advertisement, along with a copy of last week's newspaper (your personal ad can be found on page 37 of section two, I've circled it in red). You'll notice that some of the more graphic language of your ad was edited out, for which I apologize—some things are too racy even for the personals, but I think I pretty much got your idea across. Horny inmate needs women, Am I right? Please let me know if you want to make any changes.

I'm sorry to hear about the lockdown; I hope you are holding up. I'm afraid the replies I'm sending along are not going to help the time pass any better: a couple of pamphlets from religious organizations, and a postcard from a dirty old man. Hopefully something better will arrive soon, and I will certainly send along everything that comes in. In the meantime, enjoy the newspaper—the cover story is about wrongfully convicted prisoners on death row, which might be of interest.

Yours truly,
Mike Beaumier

Dear Mike Beaumier:

Hello!. This is Arthur Ratner in Meritville (inmate #B65833). We're finally off of our prison lockdown, which is a very big relief. You have no idea how much I truly appreciate your thoughtful care package of goodies, especially the very nice letter from you. It arrived just after my birthday, in the middle of our lockdown, so I was more thankful than you'll ever know.

I must tell you that I am disappointed with the responses I've gotten to my advertisement, and I'm not sure what I should do. I am only in prison for Reckless Homicide, for the time when my car went off the wet pavement and hit a tree and killed my friend, and my sentence was for two years only and I have been rehabilitated. What's the beef? I am totally free, no girlfriend or wife. I'm not looking for a sugar mama, I have plenty of my own money. And I am handsome and sexy—I am sending a picture, so you can show women and prove it, too. I wish the men would stop writing to me because I AM NOT A FAG.

Mike, I am getting out of here in August and I would like to be with a woman my first night out—it has been TWO YEARS. She don't have to be a nice girl. Do you have any ideas?

Respectfully,

Arthur Ratner

Dear Mr. Ratner:

I'm afraid that I have no letters to send you this week, but I wanted to drop a note letting you know that I'd received your letter and your picture—so many tattoos! What do they all mean? I can't make them all out in the photograph, but you look like a very handsome devil.

I know you've been disappointed with the responses you've gotten from the ad you placed with me. I warned you, didn't I? Ennui. Anyway, I've been thinking about your case, and I'm wondering if you'd be willing to entertain the possibility of hiring a "professional" for your first evening out of jail. I've enclosed another copy of the paper from last week, and if you look at page 49 in section four you'll see a listing for the kind of thing I'm talking about. They are "professional daters." I don't want to offend you in the least, and I don't know what kind of trouble this might get you in, but I thought I should put it out there. Just think about it. I've met quite a few of these women, and some of them are both nice-looking and very good people.

I am enclosing another copy of the paper for your entertainment—the nightlife columnist on page 4 of section one is hilarious this week, and she's really a great woman in person. But don't get any ideas. She has a boyfriend already.

Yrs,

Mike

Dear Mike:

Art Ratner here again. Inmate #B65833? Remember? Hello! I hope this letter finds you well. Thank you, thank you, thank you for sending me your paper, and your very nice letter. You are too funny! Do you know that? I didn't know what you meant about professional daters until I looked at the ads, and then I understood. Anyway, I thought about what you suggested and I think it might be a good idea. My parole is in five weeks and I am running out of time and I am VERY FRUSTRATED.

I looked at some of the ads, and I am hoping you can talk to some of these ladies for me and see if they are open-minded about prison inmates. I don't know if you know them personally or not, but I would like one who is pretty and not at all stuck-up, if that's okay. The ones I liked were:

Cashmere

Lola

Brittany (the first one)

Alexis

I don't know what the "TS" means in Alexis's advertisement though. What is "TS"? You can show them the picture I sent you too, so they will know I am not a freak, and they can write to me if they want.

I had to look up "ennui" in the dictionary in the library, but I don't understand why you wrote it. Are you sorry for me? I'm getting out of this place soon, so don't feel bad. Oh—I told a couple of the other inmates about you and how nice you've been to me, and I hope you aren't offended, but some of them would like to know if they can contact you for your services. I'm sending along pictures of my friends Gary (#B79556) and Nyan (#B22375)—do you have any women that might like them? Gary did a carjacking, and Nyan robbed a house. They're great guys, really.

> Respectfully,
>
> Arthur Ratner
>
> (inmate #B65833)

Dear Mr. Ratner:

Alexis is a man who dresses up like a woman. TS stands for "transsexual"—I will assume this takes her off your list.

I showed your photograph to Lola, and she says she'd rather not. Don't take it personally.

Cashmere was sort of noncommittal about the whole thing, but she said she didn't want to have to write to you. I think she might not know how to read or write, because I have to write down her ads for her.

I would like to suggest a woman named Debra—her ad (I've circled it) isn't as exciting as the others, but she's very pretty, and smart, and she thought you looked sexy. Debra's always been incredibly nice to all of us here in the office, she doesn't use drugs or anything like that, so there won't be any trouble. She'd like to write to you, but wanted to know if it was okay first. I'm going to tell her it's okay—so expect a letter from her soon.

I'm glad to hear that the guys in Meritville are such big fans, and thank you for saying such nice things about me. I was wondering why I suddenly had such a sharp increase in personal ads from inmates, and now I guess I know. You ought to consider a career in matchmaking when you get out, Arthur—you're a natural. All the guys had very nice things to say about you, by the way.

Best Wishes,

Mike

Hi Mike:

It's Arthur Ratner #B65833. Well, I'm getting out next week, and I'm all set to hook up with Deb—she sent a very nice letter with a picture, and you're right, she's hot. Thank you SO much! Deb says you've always been really respectful and nice to her despite everything, and she says if you were vouching for me it would be alright to meet me. I didn't know you were a gay (she told me) and I feel real bad for all the stuff I wrote if I ever insulted you. No offense, okay? You're a good guy even if you are a gay.

And I wanted to write to you and tell you thanks before I got out of here. Mike, you always treated me like a human being and didn't judge just because I was in prison, which means a lot. And thanks for sending all the newspapers and letters, too.

I've been saying good-bye to the other inmates here in Meritville, and I never want to see this place again. But I liked your suggestion of being a matchmaker—maybe I could set up prison inmates? That would be so cool.

Anyway—God bless you and be happy, okay?

Love,

Artie (#B65833)

[14] *The Irish Room*

SWEAT AND SHAPE. Seeking a workout partner either in
the city or 'burbs. Serious but fun, learn from each other,
motivate and support. Jogging, swimming, lifting weights,
etc. Goal is to feel good and have a meaningful workout.

Every day, by noon at the latest, I'll have usually received two phone
calls and one e-mail from the boyfriend relating the details of his morning aches and pains. There are a host of ailments—ringing ears, a feeling of being either too hot or too cold, symptoms of grogginess or
fatigue that might normally be associated with waking up late every day
but in this case can be attributed only to that Asian flu he heard about
on the news the other day—it's a veritable buffet of bad news. I occasionally make sympathetic noises and throw in a "that's terrible" or
"you should get some rest, baby," but mostly I try not to pay any attention. This is the exact opposite of what the boyfriend actually wants. I

suspect, but cannot prove, that this has something to do with not having enough brothers.

The boyfriend wants my complete attention. I am reminded of this fact often. *Are you listening? Are you paying attention?* I am not asked how my day is going, or what's going on at work, or if I'm planning to murder him and make it look like an accident. I'm expected to shut up and listen to how hard his life is. I have no choice. The boyfriend is an obvious, unapologetic hypochondriac who also suffers from actual, real physical ailments—ulcers, eczema, a mild heart condition—and the combination is noxious and exhausting.

"In sickness and in health"—that's how it goes, right? This means that your participation is mandatory in everything, no matter how gross or disgusting. When the boyfriend declares that he needs to go on yet another radical diet, it's my eating habits that change the most. I've been on Atkins, Ornish, South Beach, Body-for-LIFE, and various degrees of vegetarianism; I have been forced to give up, at different times, meat, sugar, coffee, pasta, bread, eggs, every type of dairy, and tap water. When the boyfriend frets about all the possible ways that his body might betray him, I go to the doctor and get everything checked out. My cholesterol is excellent, my body fat is low, my heartbeat is steady and strong. I box, I run, I swim, and I lift weights. I create nothing by doing this—there's no contribution to society or the greater good happening here, just sweat.

I go to the gym at lunchtime, and by the time I get back the boyfriend's on to other maladies. There will be an e-mail telling me about the bump—dare he say *lump*?—he's been frantically obsessing about since lunchtime. His back hurts. He's got a pain when he turns his neck sharply to the right, he just noticed it. If matters are urgent, he picks up the phone.

"I just went upstairs and I felt dizzy," he tells me. "A little dizzy, but I could still tell. I had to catch my breath."

"Have you eaten anything today?" I ask him.

"No," he says, "but I had six cups of coffee."

"You should go eat something," I volunteer. "You need food."

"Don't *tell* me to go *eat* something. You know it will just go right *through* me. Are you even paying attention to me? I feel crappy and you don't even *care*."

*   *   *

We all have our little hobbies. Some people go to the horse races for amusement, some indulge the urge to collect thimbles or spoons from all the state capitals, and there are those who find contentment in knitting sweaters for their cats, or creating intricate macramé planters from their very own hair. The boyfriend's favorite pastime, by far, is his health; he talks about his lower intestinal tract the way some people talk about baseball—though, of course, baseball doesn't move as fast. It's hard to live with someone whose obsessions you do not share, and many couples have come undone by the refusal of one to please just shut the hell up about NASCAR already, or the inability of one to pick up the subtle signals that his mate's interest in the breeding lines of Afghan hounds has waned. Sometimes the best a person can do is feign interest, and indulge in fascinations that they themselves find baffling. It's not easy. I often wonder how my father does it.

My dad is a simple man. A quiet man. A man whose pleasures are moderate, unassuming, reasonable, and few—Saturday afternoon football, church, a card every Father's Day, a watered-down drink on festive occasions that he can be counted upon not to finish. I'm guessing this is what Beaumiers used to be like—modest, inconspicuous, sober people, living plainly and minimally, people who did not accumulate collectibles or put on proud displays. But then my mother came along, with all her Irish crap, and changed everything.

Mom collects. Mom collects Irish. Irish *anything*. Anything with shamrocks or leprechauns on it, anything that sounds or looks even vaguely Celtic, she'll buy it and display it. We're not talking about some piddling little assortment of stuff, a couple of throw pillows embroidered with the words KISS ME, I'M IRISH and ERIN GO BRAGH or a Guinness stein. Oh, no. Those are for amateurs. For most people, green socks and an Irish Rovers CD played once every March 17 would be enough, maybe even too much, but for Mom, that's nothing, practically an insult. Mom long ago committed herself to all things Irish, or at least Irish-American, and she's not the kind of woman to half-ass anything. All of it, every chunk of Irishness, is kept together in one room—the Irish Room. No matter where my parents have lived, no matter how big or how small, there has always been an Irish Room, a place set aside for Mom's collection. It is always a very green room, as you might expect.

Every square inch is packed with overly precious knickknacks, sentimental bric-a-brac, leprechauns and rovers, and upholstered furniture awash in unsubtle shamrock prints. Mom has every Irish book, every Irish movie, every CD of bouncy or dirgelike Celtic music; there are display cases filled with Belleek china—saucers and cups, plates and bowls, bells, figurines of angels and children and animals, vases, ornaments, all of it delicate and untouchable—and Waterford crystal of practically every form imaginable. She just can't help herself. There's Leon Uris's *Trinity* sitting on a table next to the collected works of Frank McCourt; the Chieftains are playing somewhere, as they always are, the speakers of Mom's stereo hidden discreetly behind the flags and coats-of-arms from all the great tribes of ancient Ireland. The shelves are lined with history books in which The Famine and The Trouble are always capitalized, and a handy translation of Gaelic swear words lies open on an emerald-colored chair by the fireplace, by which stands a gnarled cane that was once the root of a tree in Ireland.

The overall effect is an indescribable mix of beauty and kitsch; it's all perfectly charming and utterly nauseating. The room spins. You don't know where to focus your eyes, there is so much stuff competing for attention, and it takes a moment or two before the feeling of pure, crazed, insanely happy joy bubbles up and completely overwhelms you. Some of what's in the Irish Room is expensive and precious, and some of it isn't—but I don't think that's the point. It's in there, all put together, so that Mom can have the pleasure of seeing that look spread across your face as you take it all in.

And always, standing quietly off to one side, is Dad. Watching Mom.

How does he do it? Poor Dad, a nice guy descended from nice people who were at one time French and then unexpectedly Canadian, simple people who don't collect things, never do things, avoid attention, and keep quiet. A Beaumier wouldn't obsess over aprons covered with four-leaf clovers, or figurines depicting crafty leprechauns hiding their gold from drunken potato farmers. Beaumiers aren't hobbyists, yet there's my father in every photograph, kissing the Blarney Stone for the sixth time, or lurking in the background as my mother haggles with a storekeeper over genuine, honest-to-goodness Irish linen potholders.

His jaw is set with a grim resolve, and his eyes are fixed and focused somewhere off the frame—a look that seems to indicate that Dad wishes Mom would switch to collecting stamps or motorcycles or anything that isn't green. It's the very same look I get on my face when the boyfriend tells me about that pinching feeling he gets in his neck sometimes, or how he thinks he's allergic to Styrofoam.

*SWF 47 seeking handsome knight in shining armor to whisk
me away on his white stallion to his suburban castle, complete
with white picket fence and happy ever after. I've been waiting so long for you—come rescue this fair damsel!*

I don't know any man besides me who reads wedding magazines, and I
simply can't seem to find the time to keep up with all of them. *Modern
Bride, Today's Bride, Wedding Style, Elegant Bride Quarterly, Teen
Bride, Shotgun Wedding Planner*—I really have only my lunch hour to
page through these glossy, gauzy periodicals, marveling at all the different words that somehow still just mean "white," and taking note of the
top ten reception cocktails my caterer must absolutely, positively be
prepared for.

Everybody's getting married. Isn't it exciting? There have been four
engagements in the office in the past month, and the wedding talk
is thick and constant. It wouldn't be so bad if the weddings weren't
all the result of interoffice romances—the manager of the classifieds

department is marrying one of the typists; the comptroller is marrying one of the delivery drivers; and a woman up in advertising is marrying some guy who doesn't really seem to do much of anything, his job is speculative and mysterious. He's got an office and everything, he might be the publisher for all I know, but mostly he plays video games or stands around talking sports. A couple of people in editorial are sleeping together too—though people in editorial are always sleeping with each other. I suppose somebody has to. It's not pity sex, not at all— they're writers, remember; it's *self-pity* sex. I can just imagine the sweet nothings they must whisper to each other, the tender words they share while locked in a sweaty embrace.

"Is that what you're leading with? I don't think it's strong enough."

"You're losing your point. Get on with it."

"Who are your sources?"

While it's very nice to see the people who work here choosing to pair off instead of growing old and bitter and dying alone, watching these people plan their weddings makes that other possibility seem awfully attractive. The weddings in the magazines seem a lot different from the weddings being planned around the office—there is much gnashing of teeth that not even a year's salary will buy the desired wedding gown, that guest lists are too big or too small or not done, that flowers have not been picked out, that everything is too expensive. The phone lines are tied up with mothers, caterers, and best friends calling; there are constant, angrily whispered conversations between increasingly agitated brides and their sullen grooms; and there's an air of competition among the wedding parties. *What band did you book? Are you having a DJ too? Really? Oh, I think it's important to have a DJ for after the band. It's just more tasteful. I have a list of the DJs I rejected on my desk, if you're interested.*

It's all very politely vicious, though it would be much funnier if the happy couples weren't emptying their pensions and maxing out their credit cards to pay for their wedding planners. Working for a weekly alternative newspaper is not the kind of job that lends itself to a comfortable married life; it's honestly hard to imagine anyone who works here having enough money to own a pet. There may very well be a way of living off what they pay us without starving to death, but restricting yourself to just one roommate is not the way to do it.

There's an entire world of people who have jobs that are not within thirty yards or two flights of stairs of their spouses' offices, so some of these office unions seem to smack of sheer laziness. And there's something just a little scary about being married to someone you work with—really, is there anyone in the world you'd want to spend that much time with? Who are you going to bitch about your wife to? Who are you going to complain about your husband to? If you don't get along with her mother, can you go to her boss? If he doesn't do the dishes, will it get him fired? Who gets custody of the stapler if you divorce?

I'm not sure if I should be bothered or relieved about it, but I don't think I'm going to be invited to any of these weddings, not a one. There have been excuses about logistics and locations, how it's "just family" or a "small thing, really"—but I know the real reason. They know how much I hate weddings. I only read the magazines because I'm bored and have nothing better to do. At most weddings, I am the guy outside smoking and making remarks, not taking any of it seriously, and making myself a most unwelcome guest. Which is exactly what you're not supposed to be at a wedding.

It's not that I have a problem with marriage—marriage is great; if you want to be married, go for it, I'm completely behind you. But I'm in the business of relationships, and weddings are just noise, annoying distractions, just a lot of silk, lace, and stress. I feel sorry for any woman who has had to suffer the horror of being a bride. Women are taught from the earliest age that getting married is the single biggest thing that will happen in their entire lives—ever. They've had that beaten into their heads, and once their wedding is really upon them, they realize they've been conned into worrying about every little detail, as if their entire future happiness were riding on the bows hanging off the backs of their bridesmaids' asses. The groom has it comparatively easy; as far as he's concerned, he's gonna party, he's gonna get presents, he's gonna get drunk, and, no matter how badly he behaves, he's gonna get laid. It's more or less guaranteed. But the bride—well, this is the biggest day of her life, all eyes will be upon her, and everything has to be perfect. Every day I get personal ads from women who've long dreamed of their weddings, but haven't put much thought into what kind of man they actually want to spend their lives with. There's a woman who has had her whole wedding planned out for years; she's been saving her money and has picked out a veil, and all she needs is to find some guy to stand on his mark in front of the altar. I wonder when the thought will start to creep into her head that maybe, possibly, she's been had. After the honeymoon? On her tenth anniversary? During the reception?

* . * *

As I've said, I'm bad at weddings. A bride can plan every last detail of her wedding—every moment, the placement of every flower, the length of every hair on her groom's head—but she cannot control the nihilist, cynical guest with an attitude.

When my brother Matt married his wife, Renee, it was a big show. They'd invited a lot of people, her big family and ours, and everyone was there except my brother Pat. Pat was supposed to be Matt's best man, but a strange ailment had taken hold of him, something no one was sure about, and he couldn't come—my brother Casey took Pat's place, which knocked an usher up to groomsman, which made for an empty tuxedo. And there I was.

I didn't want to be an usher. I hadn't come to this wedding to work. Of all these people, why me? But apparently it wasn't at all about what *I* wanted, no matter how hard I tried. You do not refuse a woman on her wedding day, so I put on Pat's tuxedo, which was too big, and his plastic tuxedo shoes, which were too small, and I ushered. Safety pins kept the tuxedo on me, though they were put on in such quantity and so tightly that I was hunched over; every time I attempted to stand up, another pin would snap undone and lance me. The shoes were an agonizing horror, as painful as they were ugly. I was limping people down the aisle, like Quasimodo; people no doubt thought I was the brother who'd gotten all the recessive genes. So I played it up, a gothic hunchback in wretched agony, with a limp, showing the people to their seats. Friends of the bride? *Walk this way—and beware the flower girl, she spells your doom!* Matt and Renee will probably stay married just so they never have to ask me back for another wedding.

* * *

So I wasn't going to be asked to any of these weddings—no big surprise. I was blasé about it. If they didn't want me, fine. But despite my ambivalence, I must admit I was a little excited when a fancy envelope showed up at the office, just the sort of envelope that would hold a wedding invitation.

There was no return address.

> Dear Mr. Matchmaker Guy:
>
> I wanted to let you know that because of your personal ads, I am now engaged to be married. I placed an ad in April of last year ("Shy Girl seeks Nice Guy . . .") and I got over 70 responses (!) but when I met John, I knew he was the one. I promised myself that if it worked out, I would write and thank you so you would know what a valuable service you provide. I would otherwise never have met him, since we did not live or work anywhere near each other.
>
> Thank you so very much, from the bottom of my heart!
>
> I am enclosing our wedding invitation, though I have blacked-out all the names. My husband and I are very embarrassed by how we met, and we've told everybody a dif-

ferent story. Please don't come. We hope you understand.
Sorry.

Sincerely,

Irene

P.S. My ex-boyfriend has been dating a woman for the
past four months that he met through your personals, and
they are very happy too. They tell people they met at a mon-
ster truck show.

Strange to say, this was one wedding I actually wanted to attend. I
thought about what I'd wear, what I'd say—maybe I would dress up
like Cupid, in a diaper with a little bow and arrow. Yes, I'd tell the horrified guests, it was *me* who brought these two lovebirds together—me,
me, me!—but *shhhh! It's a big secret!* Let's talk about it later, at the
reception, while we enjoy watered-down liquor and rubbery chicken.
After all, today is their special, special day.

MANIC-DEPRESSIVE WOMAN mid-40s looking for simi-
lar manic-depressive man age 30+ for movies, theater, muse-
ums, concerts, walks on the beach, walks in the park, bicycle
rides, car rides, jogging, wind surfing, sky diving, camping,
barbecues, Rollerblading, rock climbing, backpacking, travel,
volleyball, softball, baseball, football, basketball, foosball,
gardening, shopping for shoes, shopping for clothes, shopping
for food, intricate gourmet dinners, interesting and engaging
conversation, or long quiet weeks at home. Give me a call.

I came home to find a photographer, a writer, and a something that called itself a "house stylist" sitting in the bedroom, waiting for the lights to be set up. They're going to use pictures of the house in one of those magazines, *Get Home* or *Girlie Decor*, one of those glossy things full of full-page ads for European drapes made from baby seals. I tried not to scowl at the three of them, but, as they took no note of me, it hardly mattered. It's not my house and I don't get a say in it. I just live here.

"Where are your plants?" the house stylist wanted to know. The question wasn't being addressed at me, but at the house itself. "You're so—so *plantless*. How can you have all these *massive* windows and all this *glorious* sunshine and not have plants? We'll bring you some plants, baby. Some nice big leafy plants, no cactuses, nothing Santa Fe–ish, we'll put them *here* and *here,* just to frame your shot." The photographer listened and wrote things down in a little pad as the house stylist told the house exactly what was wrong with it. As the house couldn't defend itself, I spoke up in its defense.

Plants, I pointed out, were often full of bugs, and ever since the boyfriend freaked out about the ants in the powder room, plants were not welcome. The house was blameless. I was sitting on one of the footstools in the corner, where the boyfriend had put me so I wouldn't be in the way. I was soon joined by the dog, Mrs. Apples, also declared to be uncooperative and in the way. The dog and I were both annoyed by all the manic activity—the photographer's assistants, the people moving around furniture, the cables and lights and sudden appearance of magazine-friendly plants—and to unwind, we entertained ourselves by fighting over one of her stuffed toys, both of us eventually on all fours, each with one end of an acrylic duck in our mouth. The boyfriend would occasionally catch sight of us and roll his eyes, letting out a big exasperated sigh, a play-it-to-the-back-row sigh—the kind of sigh that said, "If not for this tacky man with no appreciation of American postmodern design and the big smelly dog who can't control her bladder, my life would be a print ad featuring B&B Italian furnishings and expensive kitchen appliances from Viking."

That kind of sigh.

Our house—the boyfriend's house, he owns it—was being photographed for an article entitled "Accessorize!" They weren't sure about that exclamation point yet, though I said it might be helpful when they turn this article into a smash Broadway musical. The magazine people brought in a floor lamp with a shade covered in sequins, a table sculpture made of what appeared to be bricks and broken dinner plates, a chair made entirely of Popsicle sticks, which I actually liked until I discovered it cost twelve thousand dollars. All of it was from stores and companies that advertise in the magazine. If I cared, I would have been a little insulted. Were our throw pillows not good enough for these people?

I grew up in a very nice house that no one would have ever photographed unless it had been a crime scene. I lived in that house from the time I could remember until I left for college, but my adult life has been nomadic, chaotic, and has included a lot of subcontractors. The boyfriend has owned and decorated three different homes in the time we've been together, each more opulent, more spectacular—more *more*—than the one that came before it. He moves in, rips out walls and floors, totally redoes the place until it's exactly perfect, and then gets bored and antsy to do it all again. We just get settled and suddenly we're packing boxes and moving. I carry furniture and turn off utilities while the boyfriend decorates, obsessing over the light switches in the walk-in closets, or how the color of the wallpaper in the foyer complements the wood grain of the wet bar.

I don't understand any of this, but I'm known for lacking any sense of taste or refinement. I revel in it. Until I met the boyfriend, I was content with a used futon, beanbag chairs patched with duct tape, and piles of dusty books and old magazines, all arranged in the who-the-hell-cares manner that is neither aesthetically pleasing nor terribly hygienic. If I needed light, I had my neon Budweiser sign; if I needed exercise, I had my sit-up board. To the boyfriend, this was like living in a cage lined with newspaper, with an exercise wheel in the corner.

"How did the two of you ever meet?" The writer had snuck up with her tape recorder on, and she may well have been asking about me and the dog, with whom I'd been enjoying a short postwrestle nap. She was really asking how I met the boyfriend. The truth—the actual true story—is that he drove past me in his Mercedes as I was walking down the street, rolled down his window, and offered me candy. Pretty much at that point the die had been cast; one of us had taste, money, and ambition, and one of us looked good in a tight T-shirt. The boyfriend hates this particular tale and, as with most of my stories, never allows me to finish when I start telling it, so I recommended that the writer go ask him instead, while the dog and I went back to our nap.

*   *   *

The first home we shared together—boyfriend, dog and myself—was a town house the boyfriend bought that had many lights on many dimmers, the kind of place where a person would feel at home performing open-heart surgery or landing a plane. The boyfriend's belongings arrived carefully bubble-wrapped and boxed, breakable expensive things that required insurance and worry. I carried my things over my shoulder in large garbage bags, and I took the subway. There was a disparity in income and sensibility, obviously, which we both agreed to over-

look, provided I never touched anything without asking first. Despite
this, it was a kind of honeymoon house, and we were very happy there,
in each other's company. We actually *liked* each other; he was interested in what I had to say and what I was doing, and I took pleasure
in being with him. It was a reflection of the house itself—each room
bright and open, every square foot full of optimism and excitement.
This was by design. It was impossible not to imagine cooking gourmet
dinners for two in the designer kitchen, or having intimate conversations on the spacious and sumptuous deck, or making love in the enormous master bedroom with attached sitting room and spa bath. The
actual experience, however, involved a great deal of vacuuming and
dusting, and nothing kills romance faster than housework. Eventually
the boyfriend sold the place to a young go-getter who'd made his fortune in the lucrative Beanie Babies market, buying and selling adorable
stuffed animals on the Internet to men and women I would later see at
the newspaper, placing cutesy personal ads that reeked of adorability.
The Beanie Babies guy had made so much money that he bought not
only the house but nearly everything in it—furniture, rugs, the television, even the towels in the linen closet. That none of it was actually his
didn't seem to matter to him. He was single, and lonely, and the only
women he knew fought tooth and nail over outrageously priced children's toys. If he had the house, he thought, perhaps the honeymoon
would inevitably follow.

Unencumbered by possessions or address, we took up residence
in a sort-of row house made up of tiny little dark rooms that the
boyfriend proceeded to fill with all sorts of junk—vases, club chairs,
assorted tchotchkes, various and sundry crap. Our lives were cushy,

and everything centered around the kitchen, which the boyfriend described as "Bauhaus meets Norman Rockwell." He outfitted it with every conceivable gadget and utensil, and he made extravagant meals that left us fat and drowsy. We mowed our lawn and tended the garden and waved to our neighbors and their children, and each morning I would escape to work while the boyfriend spent his days fretting over fabric swatches and color samples.

It was in this house that our fights began in earnest, over sconces. The boyfriend was torn between Naugahyde leather with paper shades or cast iron with a metal diffuser, while I adamantly held the position of not caring one way or the other. I began to wish that it would all just go away, that we'd find a tiny rental apartment—someplace small, someplace simple, just the two of us and the big dog, living meagerly but happily. Certainly, we weren't men who endlessly talked about our feelings, or shared our deepest dreams and fears, but even that would have been preferable to endlessly debating the thickness of crown moldings or the heartbreak of seamless shower enclosures. Couldn't we talk about something, anything, else? If the staircases needed lighting, why not just carry a flashlight? The boyfriend approached renovation and redecorating the way some people think about plastic surgery, always needing to "freshen things up" every couple of years or so. The backsplash in the kitchen wasn't right. The floor in the foyer didn't work. There wasn't enough beige, there was too much beige, the furniture didn't work, he couldn't live with those light fixtures in the hallway. He had already rebuilt and renovated the place twice in three years, and had somehow ended up with a house that had one bedroom and three full bathrooms, plus a powder room, just in case. You couldn't take ten steps without stumbling into a toilet. Nobody needs to go that badly.

But I wasn't the one who was paying for it—though I was often reminded that I was the beneficiary of his largesse. Look at where I was living, all these lovely things, wasn't I lucky to be so well taken care of? But I did not feel lucky. I slowly began to realize that I'd gone from kept to caught. This was not the glamorous life I'd envisioned, and it was almost a relief when the boyfriend began to scour real estate ads again. He eventually found an old power substation on the north side of the city, a rough and messy place that I thought could never, ever be clean, perfect, or precious, no matter how much money or effort the boyfriend threw at it. It sat right next to the tracks, and enormous trains roared by several times an hour, every day and every night, shaking the walls and spewing diesel fumes in their wake. The showers leaked, there were spiders and ants everywhere, and the furnace produced only the thinnest suggestion of actual heat. It was in move-in condition, as far as I was concerned, but the boyfriend had other plans.

There would be walls *here* and *here,* the windows simply *had* to be replaced, and the new furnace would be expensive but would eventually, I was told, pay for itself. How a furnace could pay for itself, I couldn't imagine. Would the furnace get a job? Did the furnace come from old East Coast money? The place was soon swarming with builders—Mexican electricians, Polish plumbers, Russian masons hauling piles of bricks in every direction, a veritable United Nations of subcontractors. And then there were the Irish carpenters, Davey and Watson.

*   *   *

Davey and Watson were paid by the hour, and they were perfectionists who took their own sweet time. Watson didn't say much, but Davey rarely stopped talking long enough to draw breath. Every few days I would stop by the construction zone to gaze, appalled, at the temple that the boyfriend was building, and Davey would rush up to me and begin his monologue.

"Yer man's in a fine mood," he would tell me, and he'd regale me with another story of how the boyfriend had lost his marbles over a wrong pipe or misplaced electrical cover. The boyfriend had appointed himself general contractor for this little project, and he was an unforgiving taskmaster. Because the Irishmen were more or less the only ones around who spoke any semblance of English, they were the ones who most often bore witness to the boyfriend's wrath. "Yer man's having a bad day," they'd tell me, or "Yer man got a wee angry at the plumber. I'd be giving him a bit of distance right now if I were you." Davey would then launch into a story about his girl in Boston, or report on his family back home in Galway, or sound off on the sorry state of American politics, television, and movies—pausing only to demand affirmation from Watson.

"Ain't that so, Wats?" Davey would say.

"Right up," Watson would reply.

It was touching that Davey and Watson would always refer to the boyfriend as "yer man." *My man.* I thought it was old-fashioned and kind of sweet, like something out of a romance novel or a Fanny Brice song. That they were usually complaining about his short temper or

demanding temperament didn't matter so much; I was the "nice one,"
after all, and I thought it was great that Davey and Watson would even
acknowledge our relationship.

"You shouldn't be so nice to them," the boyfriend would tell me.
"They get paid by the hour, and when you get them talking it's impossible to shut them up."

"They're Irish," I pointed out. "Like my mother."

"They're liars," he said. "I sent them to the lumberyard to pick up
the maple for the guest-bedroom ceiling, and they came back two
hours later saying the only wood they had was shight wood. I've never
even heard of shight wood. So I called the lumberyard and they told
me they had plenty of maple, and they didn't even know what shight
wood was."

I didn't need Mom to translate this one. *Shight,* I told the boyfriend,
was Irish for "shit." The maple at the lumberyard was *shitty.* And
Davey and Watson were famous for refusing to work with shitty wood.

"Oh," said the boyfriend, and he was quiet for a moment. Then he
shook his head and said, "Well, that's no excuse."

The renovation took upward of four or five months—how much it
cost, I didn't ask, I'm sure I would have been horrified if I knew. When it
was done, there were new furniture and new heating and cooling sys-
tems, the weeds and crabgrass had been professionally landscaped into a
vaguely Japanese garden with what the boyfriend called a "water element" but which looked to me like a puddle in a rock. There was more of
everything piled on top of everything else, to which I remained willfully
oblivious. It wasn't my money. It wasn't my house. By now I'd learned
that the boyfriend would do whatever he pleased, spend whatever it

took, and when he got bored he'd do it all over again, only bigger and grander. I tried not to think about what he might do next—French provincial meets country-western? Gothic minimalism? Would the carpeting be shag?

*   *   *

When the magazine featuring the house came out, no one was more proud than Davey and Watson. The pictures were beautiful; all their handiwork was on view, except for the bathrooms and the master bedroom.

"So, why d'you think they'd not be havin' photographs of the bath, huh?" Davey asked. "Yer man had us in there morning, noon, and night for two weeks. We put in that damn floor there twice, I tell you."

I explained to Davey that magazines don't like to feature pictures of bathrooms. They don't want the readers to imagine the homeowners sitting on the toilet.

"But why no bedroom?" Davey asked. "It's a fine room, with the pine flooring and shelves and all. Surely they couldn't have thought it weren't a fine room."

I sighed and said that probably they didn't want to feature a bedroom, no matter how beautiful or extravagant, that was shared by two men, even in this day and age.

Davey got very quiet—which was rather unusual for Davey—and poor Watson's eyes nearly bugged out of his head.

"Are you saying," Davey said, slowly, "that you and yer man are . . . That he and you . . . "

Watson let out a long, surprised whistle and rolled his eyes.

"So yer living here too, then," Davey said. "Well, knock me over, I had no idea. Why didn't you ever say so?"

"I thought you knew," I told them. "You kept calling him 'yer man' and I thought—well, I thought he'd told you."

"Not a whisper," Davey said. "Nothing. We thought you worked for him, is all, seeing's how he was always telling you to be doing this and that and how you always did it. Same as us."

I suppose I should have known. All those times they'd called him "yer man," what they'd meant was "your boss."

"So, lucky you, then," Davey said, and slapped me on the back. "All this is yours, huh?" And he flipped through the pages of the magazine, pictures of the perfect home that wasn't.

[1 7] *Mum's the Word*

YOU SHOULD DATE my dad! He's looking for a strong,
good woman 65+ with a good sense of humor for fun and
adventure. Are you a lousy cook? Who cares? Can't keep house?
Why bother? Life's too short for chores, and too short to spend
alone. Call now!

Of the many things this job requires—kindness, patience, sympathy,
the ability to survive on a meager paycheck—nothing counts as much
as discretion. Ninety-nine percent of working here involves nothing
more than keeping your mouth shut; except for when you're discussing
advertisers with coworkers, this is not the place for those who cannot
keep a secret. While everyone else gossips and speculates about the
private lives of others, you must be silent as the grave, allowing nothing
to escape your lips beyond an inscrutable yet knowing smile. Wronged
spouses will press you for information about cheating spouses, pimps
will angrily demand the whereabouts of their girls, rejected suitors will

cajole you into revealing addresses and phone numbers—but you will say zilch, zero, naught. Who, me? I don't know nuthin' about nobody.

The paper guarantees absolute privacy—no salesmen will call, no mailing list will be sold, no word of your passions and predilections will go public without a court order and a team of lawyers—but since I'm the one with the key to the file cabinet, it's my word that counts the most. I could draw a map detailing the quickest route to every eligible bachelor in town, and I know the location of every cross-dresser and spanking enthusiast in the tristate area; I have at my fingertips the means to lay waste to secrets and utterly destroy lives. To possess this power makes me deliriously happy; I won't deny it, and I'd never abuse it. Why would I? It is quite enough to know that, as I sit in my tiny cubicle, unknown and anonymous, underpaid and unappreciated, I am the most dangerous man in the city. Offer bribes, makes threats, throw tantrums—I won't talk.

*   *   *

My mother taught me to keep quiet, play dumb, and always deny, deny, deny. It is a very useful skill, especially in this job. When we were kids, the unwritten code was never give away your brothers, never turn in your sisters, and never, ever reveal confidences and sources. Except, of course, to Mom. Should you awaken to find yourself tied to your bed, your face smeared with peanut butter, Mom would know within minutes the names of the perpetrators, the length of rope used, and the expiration date of the peanut butter. The punishment, should she deign to apply one, would be the revelation of all she knew to the hapless victim, and the encouragement to strike back and strike back hard. It would have been exhausting to come up with punishments for so many unruly, constantly misbehaving children; setting us against one another was far more efficient. You'd go to her in tears, screaming bloody murder about an ice cube wedged down your underwear or a dog turd left in your sock drawer, and she'd just inhale her cigarette and listen silently until you calmed down.

"Sounds like the work of one Matthew Beaumier," she'd finally say. "My sources inform me that Matt's shown a disturbing interest in dog poop lately. Go fill his shoes with toothpaste, and call it even."

It didn't occur to any of us kids that the trouble we got into was quite often instigated by the same person who doled out the punishments that would follow. Who was it who gave us that superglue, anyway? Who suggested that there was nothing funnier than a four-year-old waking up to the horror of a homemade haircut? Who turned us on to the pleasures of duct-taping one another to stop signs, lampposts, and trees? We were patsies, dupes, controlled and watched by a malevolent force hiding behind a cigarette and a plate of chocolate chip cookies.

Escape into adulthood offered the promise of avoiding Mom's watchful eye and finally having a life, but to Mom this was just ridiculous crazy talk. This is just when things start to get interesting, she'd tell us—careers, husbands, wives, children—and she wasn't about to miss out on any of it. She never calls to ask how we're doing, what's happening, or how our lives are going. She never calls, period. She wouldn't know whom to call first, she's never played favorites, and she certainly doesn't want the long-distance bill she'd get if she started picking up the phone and calling us whenever she needed information.

We never need to catch her up on what's going on in our lives, because she already knows. She merely wants to let us know that she knows everything already—she'd have talked to one or more of her sons, who couldn't help but spill his guts about his sibling's promotion at work, the cute thing a kid had done, the new suit one bought, or the vacation another was planning.

"So, who's this guy?" she asked me one morning.

"What guy?" I replied as nonchalantly as possible. My brother Jack had met the boyfriend the evening before, so I knew this conversation was coming.

"The guy you've been seeing for the past year," Mom said, and the exasperation in her voice mocked me for even trying. "The guy your brother Jack says you're serious about. *That* guy."

"Oh, he's just—"

"He's invited for Christmas," Mom declared, and I inhaled sharply. "You can come too, I suppose, if he wants to bring you along."

"Oh, God," I stammered, "no—no, he's not ready—"

"I am," Mom said. "I don't care if he's Jewish. Tell him we always sacrifice a Jewish baby at Christmas, tell him it's an old family tradition. Be here on Christmas Eve. Or else."

I tried to warn the boyfriend. I tried to prepare him. But this was back during our early, happy times, when everything sounded like fun, and he refused to heed my dire words. He learned all my brothers' and sisters' names, and the names of their wives and children, and as we turned into the driveway of my parents' home, he had the cocky attitude of a man who thinks he's fully primed for whatever life could throw at him. All that changed even before he went through the front door, where my mother was waiting to greet him, cigarette in hand.

"I couldn't remember if your people *didn't* eat ham," she told him, "or ate *only* ham. So I made five hams." And behind her, sitting on the enormous kitchen table amid vats of meatballs, boiled potatoes, Christmas cookies, and two half-consumed turkey carcasses, were five shiny, glistening pink hams.

"You are evil," I mouthed silently to Mom, but she was already pulling the boyfriend through the door and yanking his coat off.

I could tell the boyfriend was immediately in over his head by the look on his face. He was struck dumb at the cacophony of competing conversations and arguments, and the constant antics of my nieces and nephews vying for his attention wore him down. He was appalled by the never-ending eating, and didn't know whom to root for in the resulting belch and fart contests. *I know one of you is the guy I came here with,* the look in his eyes seemed to say *but, for the life of me, I just can't tell which.*

"Never again," he said as we drove home afterward. The calm, confident demeanor he'd shown on the drive there was gone, shattered, replaced by the manic, nervous tics of someone who'd just survived a hurricane. "Never, never all of them at once. Can you take my pulse? My heart feels like it's racing. Oh, God, there are so many of you. . . ." When I called my parents to let them know we'd managed to get home safely, the conversation was brief and succinct.

"Tell him he's in," Mom said. And then she hung up.

* * *

When my mother discovered e-mail, matters got only worse. She'd spend her mornings sending us inquiries about one another, gathering detailed information, and plotting who knew what. What did I know about Colin's new girlfriend, the waitress he met at his new restaurant? Had Anne said anything about the new house she and her husband were thinking of buying? But she became especially interested in the goings-on of my brother Jack.

Jack had come to town for work, and I reported that we'd met for dinner and had a pleasant visit, even though it had been anything but. Jack arrived late, tipsy, and confided in me that his marriage was over. Really over. Things had been troubled between Jack and his wife for a long time, we all knew it, but this was a little shocking to hear. Things had reached a crisis point, he told me. Morever, Jack had fallen in love with someone else, which was at once the best thing to ever happen to him and the absolute worst. His marriage would end and it was going to be messy, it couldn't be otherwise, but he would just have to get through it.

"But whatever you do," he told me, "don't tell Mom."

It's not easy hiding things from someone who knows when you're lying, so the best I could do was to say very little. When Mom e-mailed me, asking how Jack was, all I wrote was that Jack and I had had a very nice dinner. Her response was immediate: "NICE?"

Two minutes after this came another e-mail: "CALL ME."

I wrote back, telling her that even though her use of all-capital letters was very compelling, I was at work and didn't have time to call. I put her off the next day, and the day after that, and it seemed as if she'd lost interest in the subject. But I was wrong; she was merely canvassing my other brothers and sisters, gathering evidence before putting me on the stand.

Divorce is not looked upon kindly in our family—there are certainly religious reasons for this, moral reasons, your run-of-the-mill reasons, but mostly it's because my parents don't want to deal with a constantly changing cast of characters. People were not allowed in unless we were serious about them; my parents didn't want to meet, feed, and talk to a parade of young people whom they probably would never see again. The end of Jack's marriage was a sad thing, but it couldn't compare to the fury Mom would unleash if she felt her time had been wasted.

"Just *tell her already,*" my sister Katie insisted. "She knows you know something, and she's making my life hell. She won't rest until she knows everything, so just give in and tell her."

I knew the jig was up when Mom actually called *me.* She had picked up the phone, dialed, and talked to me, in the middle of the day. At work.

"Who," she asked calmly, "is 'we'—can you tell me that?"

"I don't know what you're talking about," I said.

"Your brother," she snapped. She didn't need to say which one. "He told Pat that *we* are going to Las Vegas and then *we* might take a trip to Florida next month. And he didn't mean *we* as in his wife and kids."

I was silent.

"Mickey, who is she?"

"Well . . ." I had to choose my words carefully. "I think that's really a question you ought to ask Jack."

"That's all I need to know," she said, and the triumphant *aha!* tone of her voice was unmistakable.

Goddammit.

Every secret would eventually come out, the end of Jack's marriage would be messy and unpleasant and hard, as divorces can be, and, despite what she may have believed, Mom's omnipotence proved to have its limits. Knowledge of all things is not control of all things; she could not fix this by telling Jack's wife to turn the garden hose on him, or advising her to cut all the toes out of his socks. At work, I've learned that there's nothing so blissful, or as important, as ignorance—not just other people's, but my own. People cheat and lie, and all our lives are full of mistakes that, most of the time, we'd rather not share, and which ought not be seen. Maybe Mom finally understood, belatedly and painfully, that knowledge is sometimes nothing but hurt and anguish. Sometimes there are things that even she didn't want to know.

[18] *Salt and Pepper*

SEEKING SOUL MATE. Seeking SHM who shares my de-
votion to Jesus Christ and Republican politics, has a passion
for West Coast jazz, can recite Shakespeare from memory
(I can), thinks the Toyota Camry is the pinnacle of automo-
tive engineering (I do), shares my distaste for chick lit and
chick flicks, and agrees that finding someone just like you is
hard—but worth the wait. Contact me! We have só much to
talk about!

Matchmaking is not in my job description. I'm not entirely sure, actually, if I even have a job description—but if I do, matchmaking is definitely not part of it. They frown on matchmaking here. I'm not
supposed to get involved with the advertisers; I'm just supposed to
type their ads, dutifully answer their questions, and keep my distance.
I'm never to inquire as to whether they've met anyone, if they need
help, or if I might assist in facilitating a romantic or sexual liaison at no
extra fee. Just do your job, they tell me.

But you know, I care what happens to these people. Moreover, I get bored. A man needs a challenge from time to time, something to do that makes him feel fulfilled, something that gets him out of bed every morning and into the office, raring to go. If you spent your day sorting through the wish lists of hundreds of people, wouldn't you inevitably start matching people up? She's into travel, he's an amateur pilot; this one's into classical music, that one's into square dancing; he's a fireman, she's a pyromaniac. It wasn't long before I started to hold ads next to each other, up to the light, wondering what would happen if these two people got together. Would there be sparks, adventure, disaster? Would they settle down, come to blows? Could I be sued? I realized early on that if my suggestions were subtle and I hid my tracks, I could direct people to their one true love, or propel them toward complete and utter disaster. The possibilities filled me with a sense of moral obligation and a terrible, malevolent glee. Think of the joy and trouble I could cause. I wasn't getting paid enough to resist.

It helps that no one around here pays me much attention. Being at the bottom of the newspaper's hierarchy has its advantages, and the many layers of management above me are usually busy dealing with the delivery guys getting shot while on their paper routes, or admonishing whoever was found smoking pot in the bathroom this week. The personals don't rank high in importance, and unless something major happens—murder, grand theft auto, most felonies, and occasionally misdemeanors—I'm pretty much left to myself.

Besides, really, what harm could a little matchmaking do? It's such a sweet-sounding, old-fashioned thing, being a matchmaker, like being an alchemist or a shoe cobbler. I could play the accordion, wear a vest with a pocket watch, walk about in spats; it could be utterly adorable. The only problem with being a matchmaker is that there aren't a lot of role models for a guy to emulate. It's not a profession dripping with masculinity. The only matchmaker I've ever heard of is Dolly Levi in the musical *Hello, Dolly!*—which more or less means Carol Channing. Carol is a trouper, of course, the woman made descending a staircase her life's work, but in the real world successfully arranging a meeting between two lonely souls, while satisfying, does not warrant bursting into song and dance.

The only other thing I lack as a matchmaker is any appreciable skill at actually making matches. My early attempts were wary, well-intentioned, spectacular failures. But you can't learn to walk without stumbling first. I started by setting up people I knew in my personal life, mostly guys, and I ended up sending very dear friends out on really, really bad dates, the worst dates of their entire lives. It became clear that I didn't really know what I was doing. The end result was that I'd have two equally furious and disappointed friends, people who wouldn't speak to me for weeks and sometimes months afterward.

I thus resolved to stick to the strangers in the personals—they didn't require so much coaxing, after all, as they were already looking, and had even provided precise descriptions of who they were and what they were looking for. I thought it would be easy; it was all right there, in black and white, I would just give the people what they wanted—or at least what they said they wanted. This proved not to be as straightforward a matter as I thought it would be; the new blond girl wanted to meet that rich guy, but the rich guy wasn't interested in anyone but the Asian woman, whom I'd already successfully started off with a very nice artist.

"I'm willing to have dinner with the blonde," the rich guy told me, "but only if you let me know if things don't work out between the Asian woman and the artist—and if you run my ad for two weeks for free." A guy who wants a free personal ad is probably not as rich as he claims, which the blond girl discovered when he ditched her at the restaurant with an unpaid dinner tab. To make it up to her, I then had to set her up with anyone she wanted—and the only one she wanted was the artist.

"Well, why don't you just tell the artist that he owes you for introducing him to the Asian woman?" the blonde said, exasperated. "And you need to find a date for my friend—I'm not meeting any more of these guys alone."

"Is your friend Asian?" I asked.

"No," the blonde told me. "She's Irish."

"A redhead?"

"Reddish blond," she replied. "Very fair skin, though a little thick. Why?"

"Okay," I told her. "I'll set up your redhead, promise you coffee with the artist—no more, no less—and promise you dinner with a lawyer or doctor to be named later. But you owe me one drink with a stockbroker after work, and a walk through the zoo with a truck driver or physical therapist, whichever comes first."

Things were quickly getting complicated. My barter system was crude and messy, and it was hard to keep track of who was meeting whom. There are always several hundred advertisers placing personals at any given time, and even though I was setting up a tiny handful of them, I still managed to screw up and send some off on dates with people they'd already met and rejected. Not good, but at least people were meeting each other. There was one woman, Sandra, who lived by herself up on the north side; she was a tough case, absolutely impossible. I thought I could find her a man easily, because she had only one single requirement: she didn't like driving, she hated parking even more, she refused to ride the trains, and she couldn't stand buses. Basically, all she wanted was a man within walking distance. I set her up with every available man in her zip code, as simple as that. But no matter how close a guy was to her front door, he just wasn't close enough.

"Sheridan Road is too *far*," she'd whine. "Don't you have anybody on Clark Street this week? Or Glenwood? Someone at the corner of Glenwood and Foster would be perfect. Unless it's rainy. Or snowing outside—boy, I don't know what I'll do come winter."

It was like that all the time, but I kept at it. Juggling everyone's competing desires and demands taught me that most people don't really know what they want, and even when they do, it's sometimes the worst thing you can possibly give them. One lady told me that she wanted to meet a man of depth and thought, a man who contemplated the state of the world and his place in it. So I gave her what she asked for—a poet, a professor of literature at a college downtown. Sadly, she got him at a low point. Life, he told her, was meaningless, love was a delusion, and the best any of us could ever hope for was to die and be forgotten. He apparently hadn't gotten some grant he wanted. The evening was filled with so much pessimism, cynicism, and gloom that she still calls to talk about it, an evening she refers to as "My Dinner with Ennui."

*   *   *

Giving people what they wanted didn't seem to work, so I decided to give the people what they needed instead, which is why I began to put together couples based strictly on how attractive they were, and the likelihood that they'd have sex. And why not? Everybody's always saying how important chemistry is, that spark that ignites passion and romance. I'd size people up when they were placing their ads, and make a few friendly suggestions.

"You know who'd be perfect for you?" I'd say, and then I'd shake my head and wave off the very notion of it.

"Who?" they'd invariably ask.

"Oh, it's silly to even suggest it," I'd say. "You're going to find a lot of dates from your ad, you're so good-looking and seem really decent and everything, but there's this ad running right now, someone I know, and you'd be just so—so darn *cute* together."

It was just that easy.

I introduced the beautiful people to the beautiful people ("Cheryl's a real knockout, really stacked, and she's got this animal thing about her that's just so hot"), and with everyone else I did my best ("Gary's a really nice guy, I think you two would have some very interesting conversations"). I admit my criteria were subjective and completely arbitrary, and I don't know how people would have felt had they known their sex lives were being left to the capricious whims of some anonymous gay man in a cubicle, but at least a few people found happiness, even if it was the extremely temporary kind.

Unfortunately, there was an incident that exposed the thin line between matchmaking and merely being a pimp. I usually suggested two or three different people when I was matchmaking—the one I thought the man or woman should meet, and two backups. The back-ups were a bit of a ruse, to avoid huge expectations and the corresponding disappointments. It was easy to suggest a few different women, but I had a dearth of men who were attractive in the general sense. I didn't realize, really, how often I'd been directing women to the same two guys until one of them finally broke.

"I'm exhausted," he told me when he called to cancel his ad. "I've been on twenty dates in the past two months, and the only thing these women want is sex. What gives?"

"It's that show *Sex and the City*," I told him. "It totally changed everything." Good cover, Mickeyboy.

"I think all I want to do now is settle down," he told me. "But don't worry, I will *totally* recommend your service to everybody I know."

*   *   *

After that, I set people up based on the celebrated principle that opposites attract. It's the recipe of every screwball comedy and happy ending I've ever seen—and Hollywood wouldn't lie. Clark Gable doesn't slug Claudette Colbert in the jaw at the end of *It Happened One Night;* and in all the movies they've been in together, Meg Ryan never manages to kill Tom Hanks. Obviously, putting complete opposites together was a surefire, foolproof plan—think of all the fascinating things a devout Catholic and an Orthodox Jew could discuss over dinner, or the witty banter that happens when liberal Democrats and conservative Republicans meet for coffee. What could possibly go wrong?

In real life, opposites do not attract. Opposites don't even like to share the same elevator, let alone an evening of dinner and dancing. These meetings never ended so much as they abruptly stopped. The only thing I learned about setting up a person with his or her opposite was that it was an effective way of never, ever hearing from either of them again.

Take, for example, Mona and Kevin.

I saw Mona every day for years at my gym. She was there every time I went, morning or night, sprinting on the treadmill or pumping furiously on the StairMaster, taking spin classes and aerobics classes and Pilates and even that Iron Abs class where everyone else in the room was gay. Mona had beautiful eyes and sharp, high cheekbones—but the first thing you really noticed about Mona was her clavicle. You couldn't tear your eyes away from her bony, jutting clavicle, nor her painfully visible rib cage, nor the sticks that somehow functioned as arms and legs. Mona was a woman with some issues. She was emaciated in a way that made you immediately crave a big greasy cheeseburger with fries.

"Find someone who can take her to dinner, lunch, breakfast, even," a friend at the gym told me. "Just anything where she'll have to eat."

Mona was not enthused. The last thing she wanted was to be exposed in front of a complete stranger, and she had enough self-esteem issues. Sending her off on dates seemed almost cruel. I wasn't sure what suitable candidates I had who could handle the task. I needed a single man in Mona's age range who'd pay for dinner—it wouldn't be a very big dinner, obviously, but he'd still have to pick up the tab. He'd have to like thin women, *really* thin women, which I suspected wouldn't be a hard sell, though describing Mona as *thin* was being generous. There are plenty of acceptable euphemisms for *fat,* but very few for *skeletal*—and besides, I didn't think what Mona needed was a date so much as a good therapist.

But I'd been asked to intervene, and I couldn't resist. I introduced her to a fellow who was into adventure races—three days in the wilderness battling through the mud and rain and danger; he trained and talked of nothing else. I thought it might be a good match, as they were both painfully thin and obsessed with exercise, but they scared each other off. I sent her off to dinner with a hard-core vegetarian, a guy who refused to eat anything cooked or raised on a farm, but their separate food obsessions didn't match up. And then I stumbled across Kevin. And once the idea was in my head, I couldn't shake it. I just had to set them up. Opposites, indeed.

Kevin was sweet in every sense of the word. Where Mona was intense and driven and even a little scarily obsessed, Kevin was jolly and laid-back and easygoing. Mona got up at 5 A.M. every day, rain or shine, to go for a brisk ten-mile run, while Kevin got up at 4 A.M. to make croissants. Kevin was a big, husky pastry chef, a baker, a man of sugar and flour, and a real charmer despite the tattoos and the baking soda beneath his fingernails. He was perfectly Mona's opposite, a man who'd probably never heard of the Atkins diet and wouldn't much care for it, anyway. Kevin wrote a personal saying that he wanted a woman who was "in shape," and I decided, hey, good enough—and pretty much ran with it.

"What were you thinking?" Mona demanded when I saw her at the gym after her first date with Kevin. She was furious. "He weighs like two hundred pounds, never exercises, and cooks with shortening. All he talks about is egg yolks and Italian food and cooking with chocolate. And do you know where he took me to dinner? Carlucci's—where everything comes with pasta and they've never heard of dressing on the side."

"She was nothing but skin and bones," Kevin groused. "It was painful to even look at her. She wouldn't eat. She just picked at her food and talked about how bad carbohydrates were."

The only thing Kevin and Mona had in common was the stupid, idiotic man who'd so foolishly set them up. The whole thing was so ludicrous that they couldn't resist calling each other to report on how they'd chewed me out. It was strange, but now that they'd found a mutual interest—my hideously poor judgment, my intrusiveness, my arrogant presumptuousness—they actually had something to talk about, something to share. Last I heard, Kevin had slimmed down and Mona had fattened up, a little anyway, and they were still furious at me. But they were being furious together.

There are people who claim they have the ability to find you your one true love—buy their books, join their clubs, pay their fees, and they will look you in the eye and guarantee your happiness. You can fill out questionnaires and take personality compatibility tests, but there's no secret power to finding true love, no special intuition or can't-lose formula. The best I can do is throw as many people as I can at each other, over and over, hoping a few will end up mad enough at me to actually stick together.

NAUGHTY GUARDIAN ANGEL, WM 40, attractive, witty,
clean-cut, no bad habits, seeks sweet honey to wine, dine
and make feel fine. Pick you up, protect you, love you, fight
with you, drive you crazy and race you to old age and death.
Depending on your point of view, this plan's either perfect or
pointless.

I didn't bat an eye when they asked me who I was. The boyfriend's
door was shut, so I'd gone right to the nurses' station and asked to
speak to the attending physician. I'm the boyfriend of the gentleman in
room six, I told them—I always say "boyfriend," even though he
prefers "partner." We first squabbled about this a few years ago, in front
of the admitting nurse while he was having a heart attack, and the issue
had gone unresolved through kidney stones, colonoscopies, and high
blood pressure. I thought "partner" sounded entirely too corporate,
too white-collar, like I'd started in the mailroom and slept my way to
the top.

This latest medical crisis is probably just his ulcer, but the boy-friend's doctor finally told him that if he thought it was serious, he ought to just go to the emergency room and get checked out. Tests led to observation, and observation led to more tests and an overnight stay. I arrived just as the nurse was trying to stick an IV in him.

"Be careful," I told the nurse. "He's a bleeder. He's on a lot of blood thinners." Blood began to pour from the boyfriend's left arm, and I took his right hand and told him not to look.

Nothing pleases a hypochondriac more than being sick, because being sick means being proved right. Even though it was likely that there was nothing whatsoever wrong with him, the boyfriend still wore a triumphant I-told-you-so look on his face, and I decided to let him revel in his moment. Why should I rain on his parade? I sat with him and held his hand and told him that I was sorry, and wished more than anything that it were me there instead, getting poked with a needle and being in pain, which he knows I mean but which really isn't possible. It's easy to wish such things when you're the one who's feeling just fine.

Actually, I'm more than fine. I'm quite chipper. I'm practically perky. I'm looking forward to a quiet evening at home, alone, not pity-ing anybody. Maybe I'll pop some popcorn and enjoy the sound of no one complaining about his back or whining that his ankles hurt. I do feel sorry for the boyfriend, really I do, but he exhausts me—the wor-rying, the torment, the never-ending gloom. It's not just his health, it's his life. A typical evening consists of hearing him complain about his work, agonize about his well-being, worry about money, fret about the neighbors, and be anxious about the dark uncertainty of an unknown future. Everything, everywhere, teeters on the brink of catastrophe, and our life together is a constant state of frantic, exhausting crisis. Panic is the cornerstone of our relationship, and worry has become the glue that binds us.

I can't tell him he's wrong. The future is uncertain, disaster will strike, bad things are inevitable and impossible to avoid—but there is no proportionate response, no sense of perspective. There is a difference between the end of the world and a toilet backing up; they shouldn't elicit the same degree of angst. But when there are dirty dishes in the sink and the dog just peed on the rug—we're in a state of emergency, the threat level has been elevated to red, and nothing I say can make it go down anytime soon.

But there is no escape. The boyfriend calls every twenty minutes once I get home to report that the television in his room gets terrible reception, that the lights make noises, that people are walking around outside his room and talking, and to replay every moment of his adventure in the hospital. He *thought* he was feeling something pinching in his stomach—didn't he complain about the pinching? It started four or five nights ago, didn't it? When did he start complaining about it, on Saturday or Sunday? The nurses were nice, though—better than last time around, when they made him go outside and move his car away from the emergency room entrance; it wasn't blocking the door like they claimed, not at all.

I'm also preoccupied with an unsavory task at work, a confusing and perplexing matter, something I've been putting off for the past two days. There's been a complaint about one of the advertisers, someone I know very well, and I'm not sure what to do about it.

"She won't return my calls," the man had told me. "I'm just a little worried." A lot of people call to complain that someone they've met has suddenly turned cold to them, and I have a standardized, very sympathetic yet very firm response ready for them. I don't control the universe, sorry things didn't work out, go eat something chocolate or talk to a friend and get over it. But this guy was different. He didn't want the woman's last name, nor did he beg for her address; he wasn't looking to find her. He was worried about her. It wasn't that she'd just vanished from his life—it was more than that; she'd actually vanished from the paper.

"I thought we were really hitting it off, we'd had dinner together three times and gone to the movies and then boom—nothing, not a word. Okay, no biggie. But she doesn't even have an ad running in the personals, and she *always* has an ad in there. The same ad, every week."

"Sometimes these things just happen," I told him. "Maybe she just needed a little break. Everyone does, now and then."

"It's the one that starts 'Snappy sassy Senior seeks . . .' It's always in there. You have to know it."

"Estelle?" I exclaimed, surprised. And I was instantly horrified—I've never once, even by mistake, said an advertiser's name over the phone to a stranger.

"That's her," he said. "Married, sixty-five years old or so, living in the suburbs? She's the only girl in there who's even close to my own age."

There are two Estelles—the Dueling Estelles. One's evil, famous for eating on a man's dime and never calling men back, and the other's annoying, famous for always calling *me*. Had they switched places?

I tried to think when the last time I'd heard from Estelle Epstein was, the annoying Estelle, the one whose voice always made me wince involuntarily. I was so used to hearing that voice, and seeing her ad— all the time, every week—that I didn't even notice she was missing. Where was that shrill voice, calling *Miiiiiiiiiiiichael!* when I picked up the phone? Where was that ad of hers, the one where she says she's seeking a gentleman for companionship, movies, theater, and dinners out, but absolutely no hanky-panky unless they both feel like it?

"When's the last time you saw Estelle Epstein's ad?" I asked Andy. "Do you remember typing it recently?"

"I dunno," Andy replied. "I've typed that thing a million times. I can practically do it in my sleep. She's the only one who uses the word *hanky-panky* anymore. I always forget the hyphen."

"Her ad isn't in the paper. It wasn't in last week either, I checked. Some guy she's been seeing just called, all worried about her. The thing is, I haven't heard from her in a while."

"Wow," said Andy. "And she's always calling you."

"Not lately."

"Maybe Estelle's dead," Jeff said, popping his head around the wall of his cubicle. "I didn't want to suggest that, but it had been the first thing that jumped into my head."

"Or maybe her husband found out about her guy," Andy suggested, "and she's stuffed in a freezer in their basement."

"Nice."

"Are you going to call her?" Andy asked, and I shuddered. I'd spent so many years trying my best to avoid talking to Estelle—our conversations are one-sided in the extreme. That voice, like Gladys Kravitz from *Bewitched,* but on speed. It made my stomach churn.

"I'm going to try to avoid it," I promised.

*   *   *

I wasn't *worried* about Estelle. I didn't even like Estelle. I didn't like *either* Estelle. I might very well hate all the Estelles in the world. One was a heartbreaker, taking men for a ride, spending their money and then dropping them like used Kleenex, obviously unable to commit and apparently never wanting to be known by any man. The other cheated on her husband and called me constantly. Why should I worry about either one of them? They were both perfectly horrible. Were they my responsibility? So maybe Estelle Epstein's personal ad had gotten her into a little trouble. That wasn't my fault, it wasn't my problem. I didn't have any obligation to her, even though she had placed an ad with me every week for the past six years, had phoned probably thousands of times, and knew me by the sound of my voice as surely as I knew her by the sound of hers. Besides, what was I supposed to do? I wasn't going to call. But then I changed my mind. Then I changed it back again. What if her husband picked up the phone?

"Hello?" Estelle had picked up the phone on the first ring.

"Uh, hey, Estelle," I said haltingly. "It's Mike from the paper." There was a long silence. "Uh," I stammered, "I just wanted to know if you're okay, if everything is okay. Because—"

*"Miiii-*chael*!"* Estelle shrieked. "You are *such* a sweetheart to call.

Oh, you *missed* me, did you? You are *so* sweet to call and check in on me. I can't tell you how *much* this means to me."

"Well," I said hastily, "okay. You sound okay, then, so—"

"Now, *why* would you be worried about little *me*, of all people?"

"I just noticed your ad hasn't been in the paper lately, and I didn't—"

"Oh, *that*," Estelle said. "I've just been *terribly* busy, I was practically *aching* for a break anyway. You *know* how the gentlemen can be, always wanting to go do dinner and dancing and *everything*. But how sweet that you noticed I'd gone missing. Honestly, I was beginning to think you didn't *care*."

"Well, I wasn't the only one," I told her. "It's none of my business, but there was a guy, a gentleman, I mean, who called here the other day, someone who met you who was worried because he hadn't heard from you."

There was a tense silence on the other end of the line.

"Was it Roger?" Estelle asked. Her voice was low and filled with seriousness. "Was it Tom? It was either Roger or Tom. Or Peter?"

"He didn't tell me his name."

"It couldn't be Avery," Estelle growled. *"He* hasn't called in months." Her voice suddenly came back to its old singsong chirpiness. "It doesn't matter. Some gentlemen just get *too* attached, you know. And I'm afraid I just don't want that kind of attachment. I can't—"

There was a terrible, halting choking noise on the other end of the phone.

"Right now I just can't—it just won't—" And her voice trailed off into silence.

It got very quiet on the phone, neither of us saying anything.

"Are you there?" I finally asked. "Is everything okay?"

Estelle took a long, hard breath.

"I certainly don't want to—I wouldn't, you know, intrude on your life," I told her.

"I had to put my husband in a nursing home last week," Estelle said. The way she said it sounded like someone ripping off a bandage, quick and abrupt. "Mort's in the late stages of Alzheimer's, the terminal stage. Did I tell you my husband had Alzheimer's? It just got impossible to keep taking care of him at home. Oh, it's not unexpected, we both knew from the beginning that this was the way it was going to end up. I just needed to take a break and get everything in order around here." She laughed a little laugh—not her normal, overly coquettish forced giggle, but something that sounded tired. A hard laugh.

"Oh, Estelle," I said. "I'm so sorry. I never knew."

"I never told you," she said. "I don't want people to think of me as 'poor old Estelle' and feel sorry for me, taking care of her crazy old husband. I've felt sorry enough for myself, I don't need any help. Oh, it was hard at first, when we both knew what was happening, my husband and I. You feel like things are being stolen from you left and right, and you can't do a thing about it. We had so much stolen from us, Mort and I, everything. Now I don't even have him here. It's a terrible disease, Alzheimer's, just terrible. But what can you do? You can't live like that forever, under a cloud—at least *I* certainly couldn't. There is just so much grieving you can do before you simply have to stop. And Michael, *I* absolutely *refuse* to stop living."

I was speechless.

"Now, don't you cry," Estelle said. "There is *nothing* to cry about. I'm fine, and you can tell all my gentlemen callers that I'll be back in action in no time. It's just that right now the house feels so empty—you get so used to your life being a certain way that you miss it when it's gone, even when it's awful. And I just want to sit here and miss it for a while."

"Okay," I told her. I was a little pissed that she could tell that I was crying, and I tried my best to sound nonchalant. "But you know—call me if you need anything." I was horrified at the words coming out of my mouth. Somewhere in my brain a voice was screaming, *No! You fool! Take it back immediately!*

It was Estelle who told me the most important, truest thing I've ever heard about relationships. She was talking about her own situation, but I knew it applied to mine as well.

"Love," Estelle said, "real love, is when you realize that you're in a race to see which of you is going to die first. And the worst thing in the world is when you lose."

[2 0] *Poetry, Slammed*

She'd never been married
She'd never been kissed
They said if she waited
No man could resist.
The problem is this:
She's fifty.

The lines above are not my own
I don't know whom to credit
But perfectly they set the tone
Pretend it's me who said it

Her name, unmentioned will it be
We won't engage in blackmail
Protect her anonymity
But tell the juicy detail

In want of a someone
Strong, handsome and "nice"
The details were sketchy
But her goal precise:
The tossing of rice
Rolling dice

She listed all her wondrous traits
Her dreams and aspirations
In hopes of turning casual dates
To formal conjugations

She wrote of stars and flighty things
Rainbows, butterflies, and birds
A unicorn equipped with wings
Somehow figured in her words

Her language was gooey
What made matters worse
The words were in stanzas
She'd done it in verse
My bane and my curse
Are poets

Poetry has its time and place
Tombstones mostly, I suppose
Below we lie in death's embrace
While above words decompose

But love is neither angst nor sweet
Torment nor saccharine sighs
Poems are for love in defeat
Or for love that's yet to rise

I sent back her verses
With a stern lil' note
"No poetry welcome"
I happily wrote
I don't want to gloat
So I won't

Free-verse rhymes are not the trouble
'Tis poets where the problem lives
Trapped inside an angst-filled bubble
Using stupid words like *'tis*

Our lady threw a total snit
Her rights I was denying
I let her have her hissy fit
And didn't bother replying

But gaze upon this page
And my point you'll see
How much space goes wasted
How few words you see
Printing poetry

[2 1] *The Dog Walker*

TROPHY DATE WANTED. Cute SWF 23 seeks tall buff guy
23–27 who can shake it on the dance floor for office Christmas
party. No funny stuff, I just need a dance partner and some-
one to sit next to at dinner so I won't look pathetic in front of
the boss.

The best thing—the beauty of it, the genius—is that the only utensil
you need to make, serve, and eat dinner is scissors. There are no pots
and pans, no plates, you don't even need silverware. You just run the
package under hot water (room temperature works if you're in a
hurry), cut it open, and eat. Well, suck. Suck and chew—it's pretty
mushy, so don't worry, there won't be much chewing. Some of the bigger chunks, they could be marshmallows or possibly potatoes, those
might need a little chewing. Read the package to be sure; it'll give you
something to do while you're eating. There are aisles and aisles of
these glorious, fully prepared meals in the supermarket, no-fuss food
to be eaten over the kitchen sink by people who live alone. Since the

breakup, I've been living on a diet of these bachelor dinners, a regimen that's about as healthy as it sounds. The only fiber I get is from smoking cigarettes, a habit I indulge in around the clock, now that there's no one around to throw me baleful, critical looks.

Bad diet, smoking, drinking, staying up late—I'm completely incapable of taking care of myself, now that I have only myself to take care of. I used to be motivated, conscientious, and dependable, but on my own I am utterly inept. There is no one to do things for, no one to demand all my attention or require all my effort, no one whose bottomless neediness at least provided some purpose for me. I couldn't take it anymore, I just couldn't, but I didn't plan ahead. I have no idea what to do with myself now.

I'm talking about the dog, of course. I can't believe how much I miss her.

There was no question as to who would get her. She was the boyfriend's dog, she loved him more, they were best pals. When he was around she was always with him, and when he was gone she'd lie by the door until he came back; she would lie next to him in the bed at night, all one hundred pounds of her, resting her head on the small of his back as he slept. They would chase each other until they were both panting, and wrestle together until the floor was covered with drool. The dog would rarely play this way with me. I was not the fun one; I was merely the other one, the one she'd come to when she needed something. She would get into my line of vision and stand perfectly still, waiting for me to notice her. She wouldn't bark or whine, she didn't need to; her eyes would say it all: *Now.*

There were slight variations between *feed me now* and *gotta take a crap now* and *wash my filthy toys now,* but I knew how to discern each from the others. I could also intuit the degree of immediacy—there was *now* and there was *right now.* The dog and I had an understanding. I was the one who fed her, pooped her, peed her, bathed her, and shoved pills down her throat, and she in turn would begrudgingly accept my assistance. When she was sick, she would come to me and press her head against my leg, demanding sympathy and sweet words, which I gave in abundance. When there was a thunderstorm and she was scared, I'd let her pile her massive bulk on top of me as I sat in my chair, my arms barely reaching around her as I softly reassured her. She was, as I said, the boyfriend's dog, but when she needed me she knew I would be there for her, to take care of her. These were the little moments when she was mine.

There had been happy, carefree times, of course—when we were young and new, puppies in love, all three of us. But things changed. Nearly simultaneously, both the dog and the boyfriend got sick; she had this terrible autoimmune disease that caused her to incessantly bleed, pee, and shit, and he suffered a heart attack that left him weak and incapacitated for months afterward. It was a very dramatic time, and I had no idea if I was up for the challenge.

I hadn't ever taken care of anyone before. It was nothing to let my own life slide into chaos, indulging in bad habits and unhealthy behaviors, running from one lousy, low-paying job to another. But I was responsible for this man and this dog; they both needed special diets, multiple expensive medications, and constant attention. And although I was frightened—so frightened of messing things up for them that, even now, I can instantly recall the feeling of overwhelming terror—

I never let either dog or man see it. Dogs can smell fear, you know. We would get through this, I told them. And though I had no idea how, I meant it.

I spent every moment I could with the boyfriend in his room, sitting in a chair by his bed while he slept or fretted. When his family came to visit him, no one asked who I was or what I was doing there; with the exception of his mother, I'd never met these relatives before, and they knew nothing of me—although I knew all about them. The boyfriend's uncle, aunt, and cousins were all very nice people, but they'd been kept in the dark about the life the boyfriend shared with this not nice, non-Jewish nongirl. Apparently at one point, the uncle cornered the boyfriend's mother and asked just who the strange little man was, the one who was always sitting quietly in the corner of the room.

"Oh, *him*," the boyfriend's mother replied. "That's just the dog walker."

I actually *lived* in the house—but this didn't seem like the time or place to go about asserting myself. No one seemed to wonder why the dog walker would be keeping a constant bedside vigil; no one suggested that my time might be better spent maybe actually walking the dog. Everyone probably understood who and what I was, but the charade was easier to live with, under the circumstances. I wasn't righteously indignant or offended; I'm not built that way, and at the time, I had more pressing issues to attend to. More than anything, it provided something for me to laugh about during a time when I really needed it.

Besides, I *was* the dog walker—and the housekeeper, and the pharmacist, and even the chef, despite my complete lack of kitchen skills. Luckily, the boyfriend and the dog both required diets that could generously be described as "bland"—boiled this, mashed that, any food that was mostly gray in color and utterly lacking in taste—and never was I more grateful to be an even worse cook than my mother. The dog and the boyfriend would spend the day together in bed while I washed her blood and urine off the floors and folded his laundry. I'd run off to the store to get him the magazines he wanted, or a new toy for her, and then the three of us would walk down to the corner for exercise—he in his bathrobe, his steps slow and deliberate, she at his side, equally lethargic, and me between them, holding a hand and a leash.

It went on like this. The dog would get better, then worse, then better again. The boyfriend got stronger and stronger, but so did his worries—a big thing had happened to him, a major event, and he had suffered, but the result was that every little ache and pain now sent him into an obsessive, all-consuming panic. And I'd become the caretaker, the listener, the support. And the patsy.

It's good to be loved for something. Everybody needs to feel needed, but there's a point when one hungers to be seen as something more than just the man who takes you outside to pee. I didn't mind any of it for the longest time; I did what I thought I was supposed to do, made the sacrifices I had to make, and didn't think twice about it. But somewhere along the line, at some moment that I can't exactly pinpoint, my gallantry became a raging martyrdom, a psychosis, a thing straight out of Ibsen.

It was a shock when I left. The guilt was overwhelming, but it could not be otherwise. I had gone from being selfless to being a man with no sense of self at all, a collection of tasks performed and services rendered that, in the end, didn't add up to anything. Nothing I did could ever make the the dog happy; no amount of care would make her love me. And once I realized all this, I couldn't pretend I didn't know.

The boyfriend—the ex-boyfriend—didn't call me when the dog got sick, and I wasn't with her when she died. I should have been. Had she forgotten me? Did she miss me? Had she wondered where I'd gone? I had been her protector for such a long time. She died in his arms, they were together but they were alone, while I sat in my tiny apartment, greasy and stinking of cigarette smoke, eating food not fit for a dog.

HEY VALENTINE REJECTS! You are not losers, no matter what anyone thinks, not as long as you keep your chin up. SWM still isn't sure who he is or what he's looking for, but won't quit looking still hoping until he finds it. There's someone for everyone. I know you're out there—I'm out here, too.

I hate Valentine's Day. *Hate.* It's not just that the desperation of the lovelorn rises to a frantic, maudlin crescendo—though that's bad enough; what's worse is that this happens in the middle of February, in the darkest days of winter, a season more appropriate to suicide than to romance. Who decided to put this holiday here, of all places? The city feels like the bottom of a cold, wet cave; everything is gray and damp and unfeeling; the sky and earth and people are all the same shade of smudged, depressing, lifeless gray. Despair hangs frozen in the air, and winter feels like it will never, ever end.

Winter is always my favorite time of year, my favorite season. But then along comes Valentine's Day to spoil everything with its whorish shades of pink and inane romantic gibberish, its absolute insistence that you simply must, *must* be in love. It's a pushy little holiday, designed to make you feel obligated if you're in a relationship or inadequate if you're single, good only for flower shops and greeting-card companies—and, of course, the personals. It's our busy season, our Christmas blowout and going-back-to-school sale all in one, and the workload is staggering. Jeff and Andy are too busy even to complain about how busy they are; I occasionally stand on the chair in my cubicle to make sure they're still there, and I wait until one or the other of them notices me looking and gives me the finger.

I'm told this will be the last Valentine's Day of manic customers and long hours. Next year, they say, everything will be different; everything will be done on computers, on the Internet, and life will be easy and carefree. There won't be any typesetting, or inscrutable handwriting, or crazy people coming in off the street bawling in loneliness, demanding that I dig into the bag of happiness I surely have hidden somewhere in back. There won't be any mail to open, no phone calls to take. There will be a screen and a button, and that's all. I'll be completely invisible, anonymous; there won't be any human interaction, no connection with the people placing personals or the people answering them. Everything changes and moves forward, and things will not be the same—but for now, it's gray and cold, time itself seems frozen, and I hope it goes on forever.

I'm not in the mood for Valentine's Day. I've completely isolated myself since the breakup. I wake up each morning, go to the gym, go to work, return home, and immediately crawl into bed. There are no wild nights out at the bars, no dates, no adventures. Friends no longer call to leave messages that are never returned—even my family has backed off, knowing that I have to have some space, and respecting my desire for silence. I need this. I want to be alone; I don't need to be cheered up or given pep talks; I don't want to hear that I'm handsome and kind and sweet and that I'm going completely to waste, and that I should get out there and enjoy myself. I don't want to be around people. People are the problem. Right now, the only thing I have to look forward to, if forced to deal with humanity, is having a button that I can push to reject them. I plan on pushing that button a lot.

I was like this after my last breakup, years before, hiding myself away like a hermit. I went into a period of seclusion until I woke up one morning to the realization that I'd been alone, and inadvertently celibate, for almost two years. Maybe it's a Catholic thing, or a middle-child thing, but it's definitely, at heart, a petulant thing, like a child holding his breath to get attention. But being aware of this tendency doesn't prevent it. I'm going to have to go through a dark period, and I will just have to let it play itself out.

Everything will be better after the Valentine's Day party. Every year the paper throws a big singles party on February 14, an event that Andy, Jeff, and I begin dreading in December. There is no budget for these affairs; they're usually held in semi-decrepit nightclubs and draw only the dregs of society, the worst of the worst. Last year we got fourteen men and two angry, unbalanced middle-aged women—the Sumos, of course—who wore Valentine's dresses made of red and pink crepe paper held together with tape.

"You call this a *party*?" one Sumo snarled when she walked through the door. "Where's the *food*?" The fourteen men turned on their barstools, regarded the new arrivals, and wisely opted to go back to their drinks.

The Sumos stared at the backs of their heads for a long, crazy moment, and finally one turned her gaze on me, standing at the door, a clipboard held to my chest, eager with anticipation of disaster, excited about what cruelty the Sumos might let loose. Would they punch, spit, tear their craft-project dresses off their squat little bodies and run through the bar naked, screaming about the cruelties of being middle-aged single women with no prospects?

"This party is for *losers,*" one said. And with that, the Sumos turned around and left. They had been there for less than thirty seconds. They were, by default, the belles of the ball.

It's never good for your ego to be called a loser by short, ugly, fat women who make their own clothes, but at least last year I could be silently smug about it. After all, I had someone to go home to, didn't I? Even if things had been awful between us, with the fighting and the separate beds and the constant tension, at least I wasn't single—right? This year, I had no such lie to tell myself. I would find myself in a bar with a handful of sad, lonely, hopeless people, men and maybe even a few women, all of us waiting for something, anything, to walk through the door to save us. I would merely be one more of them.

They will complain about the personals, no doubt, and how no one seems to be answering their ads anymore because everybody's on the Internet—and I will nod and agree with them and tell them all about the changes we're making, and reassure them that next year things will be different. But we are all getting older, and we all have suffered losses and carry scars, and maybe we should just accept that the promise of all we could have been and could have held has been lost. I don't want to be around these people, because they will instantly recognize the despair in my eyes as their own—and if I didn't believe in the possibility of love, who could?

"Who are you taking to the Valentine's party?" Jeff asked me on the subway after work.

"Nobody," I replied. "I'm working. So are you."

."I'm bringing Stephen and Carl," Jeff said. Stephen is Jeff's current boyfriend, and Carl is his ex. Theirs was one of those friendly, immediate breakups that twenty-somethings manage to have; it's easy to break up with someone you've dated for only six months or so. "You should ask someone. Andy's even bringing his new girlfriend."

"I don't know anyone," I told Jeff.

"You have to know *someone,*" Jeff said. "Everyone knows someone."

"Nope."

"Why don't you take out a personal, then?" Jeff said.

I made a face.

"No, seriously," Jeff said. "Really. Why don't you? You ought to, and you know all the tricks. Even if it's just for laughs, it's better than moping around. You've been no fun at all lately."

"Thanks."

"Andy and I will write one for you, what do you think?" Jeff suggested. "We'll put in that you're this big, hung, insatiable muscle stud—"

"Which is true," I agreed.

"Who's a little moody because he hasn't gotten any in a while, though you're generally a little moody even when you have, and that you're looking for a nice guy to buy you dinner—"

"No," I said. "Not dinner. Never dinner. You don't want to get stuck across a table from some mess for an entire meal. Coffee. Not dinner."

"Coffee, then," Jeff said, exasperated. "Let them buy you coffee, jewelry, whatever, I don't care. But you're going to write a personal ad."

In seven years I've cranked out hundreds of personal ads for other people, but never one for myself. Never had to. I never really gave it any serious thought, and it wasn't until I sat down to write one that I realized just how difficult it is. You need to give out certain inalienable facts about yourself—your age, your color, what your body looks like—but the rest is all mush and conjecture, and you have to present it all in a way that's both efficient and memorable.

SWM, I wrote—and then I got stuck.

"I can't do this," I told Andy. "This is stupid."

Maybe I wasn't ready yet.

"Let's see," said Andy. "You could put something in about your shitty job and low pay—you homos think that's hot, right?"

"Shut up," I said. "So who's the new girlfriend?"

"You'll meet her tonight at the party."

"How'd you meet her?" I asked. "Did you place a personal?"

Andy threw me a look as if I was crazy.

"Hell, no," he said. "That's for losers."

I crumpled my ad in my hands and threw it in Andy's garbage can. To hell with *this.*

*   *   *

There were already people waiting for us when we got to the bar—the two who are always waiting for us when we have these parties. Year after year, no matter where or what, Big Baby Man and the Old Coot are there to greet us. Jeff, Andy, and I love the Old Coot, who's sweetly daffy and much more interested in seeing us and catching up than in dating. Big Baby Man is another story. Throughout the year I talk to him by phone, and I'm always surprised on Valentine's Day to find that he looks exactly the way he sounds—sweaty, disheveled, and whiny. The guy calls to complain about everything, literally everything, though rarely anything to do with the personals. I have had long conversations with him about the sorry state of the government, the rapidly decaying ecosphere, the looming economic threat from the Chinese, and why all the women who won't date him are stuck-up, rotten goddamn bitches.

Mostly people came in and sat alone. Two women showed up, turned around, conferred with each other, and then reluctantly came in. It was a very cold February night, the wind was howling, and I suspected the turnout was going to be even worse than last year's.

But then an extraordinary thing happened.

A couple—a man and a woman, clearly together—walked in and sat at the bar. They ordered drinks and sat together, not saying anything at all, just sitting and leaning against each other, looking across at themselves in the mirror behind the bar. The woman looked a little like she'd been crying, and the man seemed lost in thought, and they wore quiet smiles on their faces. I watched them as they watched themselves in the mirror behind the bar, and it was as if I could read their thoughts. *We look good together,* they were thinking. *We belong together. This is right.*

"That guy just asked that woman to marry him," I told Jeff. I just knew this, I was sure. "Look, over there, the two at the bar."

"Congratulations!" Jeff yelled out to them, and the man and woman were jarred awake from their dreamy reverie. The man bowed his head in embarrassment and the woman beamed, and when she held up her left hand to show off her engagement ring, the crowd burst into applause and cheers.

It must have been a little strange for them, to have a roomful of singles come up to shake their hands and congratulate them. I would have expected there'd be a little jealousy, but there was none, not even from me. It was sweet to watch them together, having a drink before going off to a celebratory dinner, and then phone calls to parents and friends, and the rest of their lives together. Who knew how it would all turn out for them, if they'd be together until the end? For now, at the beginning, they were together. And for now that was enough.

I thought about the happy couple on the long subway ride home, how excited they seemed and how oblivious a person in love has to be to the things that can go wrong. And I thought about all the people at the party, mostly guys and even—not only—a couple girls, and it occurred to me that maybe my family was even bigger than I knew. I thought about these things, and I watched the people on the subway, all potential matches, all potential ads. And for the first time in many months, I wasn't preoccupied with regret or loneliness, but with a tiny sense of hope. It might have just been gas—the food at the party was terrible—but no, it was definitely hope.

I know I'm in here, not asleep and not lost, maybe a little harder but maybe also a little wiser. We're all suckers, as Andy and Jeff like to say—

but we're *all* suckers together. My last love affair didn't work out—many don't, but the next one might, and, if not, maybe the one after that. There may not be someone for everyone; there may not be a God in heaven, or peace on earth, either. But that doesn't mean you just sit around at home doing nothing. It's cold outside, but you have to love winter, all of it, the snow and the gray—because eventually winter always ends.

I got home, and though it was late, I sat down at my desk and began to scribble words upon the page. *SWM seeks,* I wrote—and then I just kept going.

Acknowledgments

I would like to thank my editor, Carrie Thornton, for her patience and skill, and for calling me "doll" and "knucklehead" when the need for either arose; and my literary agent, Randi Murray, for her persistence and faith, and for never forgetting she was a lady even when I was telling her the dirtiest stories.

A big shout-out to Brett Murphy and the classifieds department at the *Chicago Reader,* as well as to the fine waiters and waitresses at Augie's Diner on Clark Street, who kept me fed and watered throughout these proceedings. I'm indebted beyond words to Jonathan Goldstein, Starlee Kine, Jane Feltes, Diane Cook, Todd Bachmann, and everyone at *This American Life* for their encouragement and their spicy brains.

Thanks to Todd Combs, Dennis Wierl, Dan Wangler, Mark Hantoot, Dan Santow, Andy Hermann, Jeff McMurray, Brandi Bowles, and Daniel Rembert for his great design. Steve Eck held my hand every day through this, and Todd Barone got everything else. My gratitude especially to Steven Barclay, David Sedaris, and, of course, D.R.

About the Author

Michael Beaumier enjoys long walks along the beach, bacon and eggs, and getting paid. He has written humor for the *Chicago Free Press, Windy City Times,* and other publications, and has made frequent appearances on *This American Life.* He lives in New York City.